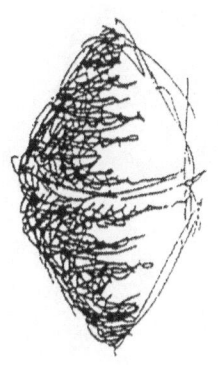

Also by Maurice Scully

Books
Love Poems & Others
5 Freedoms of Movement
The Basic Colours
Priority
Steps
Livelihood
Sonata
Tig
Doing the Same in English
Humming
A Tour of the Lattice
Several Dances
Play Book

Booklets
Prior
Certain Pages
Over & Through
Prelude, Interlude & Postlude
Tree with Eggs
Work
Game On

Art Object
Numbers [with Coracle Press]

e-chapbooks
Five Dances
Rain [signed piece]
Plays

CD
Mouthpuller

Children's
What is the Cat Looking At?

Maurice Scully

*Things
That
Happen*

Shearsman Books

First published in the United Kingdom in 2020 by
Shearsman Books
P.O. Box 4239
Swindon
SN3 9FN

Shearsman Books Ltd Registered Office
30–31 St. James Place, Mangotsfield, Bristol BS16 9JB
(this address not for correspondence)

www.shearsman.com

ISBN 978-1-84861-712-4

Copyright © Maurice Scully, 1987, 2001, 2004, 2006, 2020.
The right of Maurice Scully to be identified as the author
of this work has been asserted by him in accordance with the
Copyrights, Designs and Patents Act of 1988.
All rights reserved.

ACKNOWLEDGEMENTS
5 Freedoms of Movement was first published by Galloping Dog Press in 1987,
and then in a revised edition by etruscan books, 2001.

Livelihood was first published complete in one volume by
Wild Honey Press, Bray, Co. Wicklow, Ireland, in 2004.
Parts of the whole had previously been issued in pamphlet or e-chapbook
form by etruscan books, Form Books, hardPressed Poetry, Longhouse,
Poetical Histories, Smithereens, Staple Diet, Tel-let and Wild Honey Press.

Book-length extracts from *Livelihood* were previously published by
Pig Press, Reality Street Editions and Writers Forum.

Sonata was first published by Reality Street Editions, Hastings, in 2006.

Tig was first published by Shearsman Books, Exeter in 2006.

The drawing of flying birds on p. 97 is by Leda Scully, then aged 8

Grateful thanks to all concerned.

Contents

5 FREEDOMS OF MOVEMENT

Unauthorised Credits / 15
Instances / 25
A Record of Emotion
Side A / 37
Side B / 47
Two Caterpillars / 65
One Wallflower / 81

LIVELIHOOD

Prelude / 99

The Basic Colours

I think yes / 113
On Site: A / 115
So let me / 131
On Site: B / 133
ah whoom! goes the orchestra / 143
A tree beside some water's / 149
(History) / 155
/the Police are perfect / 159
And then I woke up / 161

Zulu Dynamite

The Pale Blue Jotter / 169
The Black Notebook / 179
The Yellow Logbook / 187
The Red Notebook / 201
The Dun Copy / 211

Priority

Prior / 219

Interlude / 229

Over & Through / 241
Coda / 267

Steps

I / 275
II / 291
III / 305
Coda / 325

Adherence

ABC / 339
Cohering / 355
DEF / 377
Coda / 385

Postlude / 393

SONATA

I / 425
II / 449
III / 467
Coda / 495

TIG

Stepping

I
[Blessing the Animals] / 515

II
[Backyard] / 521
[Waterway] / 524
[Backyard] / 529

III
[A Falling Leaf] / 537
[Picking Persimmon] / 539

Coda
[A Place to Stay] / 547
Sonnet / 550

Coda Coda
Sonnet Ode: Blessing the Animals / 555

Bread

I / 565
II / 571
III / 579
Coda / 585
Coda Coda
[A Place. To Stay] / 599

Notes / 607

: in Sumerian pictographs thought to mean *legal* or *decision* or *trial* or *peace*

Five Freedoms of Movement

Unauthorised Credits

An old house   absence of sound   trees
moss   wildlife   that feeling of surface
over surface with smooth spaces between
inside/busy   the sky in the sky
in the stream   moving
sunshine after long rain and a rich smell
rising from the steam
from the grass
a propeller on a wooden frame
taking a breeze's fancy over a hedge
in a field
nobody for miles
except   one thin white line
trespassing slowly   across vast blue

right forefinger held over left forefinger
and holding right lace under left,
left forefinger to switch left lace under right
connecting right thumb compleating a twist;
then forefingers and thumbs of both hands to pull both lace ends
in opposite directions with equal force: there, movement one.
Now right forefinger to press on the twist,
left hand propels left lace to right forefinger
slips around laceloop passing to right thumb
left thumb pushing through looplet under loop one
to waiting right thumb, which pulls.
Finally, both right and left forefingers and thumbs to grip again
giving shape, and pull in opposite directions with equal
force and this time still equally, but also, for form,
down: end of second movement, first foot.

It is disappointing to note that you have not responded to a previous communication in connection with your account and that you are continuing to avail yourself of unauthorised credit.

When
    waiting begins
             begins and
rain drops to the rooftop
that rose to meet it
in the first place   yours
you find yourself rising – rising –
  through time-tables
     condescension in the corridors
        interconnected room-theories underground – to go –
go – the baby in the cot
caught waiting in the first place
one and multiple,
calling, breathing, abating,
recalling, making that brief space breathe;
for you, encircled, wide-eyed, moved.
Cling to the lattice.

Where a building is broken away
a broken support juts
held down-pointing by three floorboards
broken at that point
and shadows against the wallpaper
that once just
and under a brick cavity
where a fireplace in a first-floor room
kept maybe
the place warm.

Unless payment, with interest to date of payment, is received within ten days from the date of this letter, proceedings for recovery will be instituted against you without further notice.

The soft down in the soft shadow, bright brown
eyes, upcurled lash, smile scherzo but frail as
the head tilts sideways casual even a bit/packing
letters, stamped ends this way, to rotate on the
belt the bones of the neck and jaw showing the skin,
the tactility of the dance of ideas enveloped by a
slower, bigger body-dance, quite small, sluiced, so many
units that spark in the interplay attach to the memory-
end: sliver of the True Cross, the Virgin's Milk, one
phial, existent places, imagination (dog at large)
addressed to pulped into to stylized and repetitive
observance, Hardstone St, Wine St, Paradise Row, Misery
Hill, round and round, stamp your feet! they go around,
spaces in people's lives not gaps from post to post
sorted and evaporating under a pressure: I know I
can't preach but I did think, Pigeon, I was quite under
the franked impression, the squeal and the blare and
the tweedle, through quaint corners of this look
I think I wait! I……

mania: an abnormal elation
with overactivity and lack of insight.
The patient talks continuously, makes puns,
has euphoria and insomnia, is cheerful, arrogant and interfering,
has flights of ideas one running into the next
but easily distracted and seldom finishes anything
s/he starts; lack of control may lead to alcoholic
and sexual excesses, obscene conversation
and attacks on others.
There may be delusions of grandeur.

A brick or two against that broken door to keep my little daughter out.
There. Rain. Twilight. That sound of traffic on wet streets
some streets away sending a delicate intertexture
of intermittent sound intact this far. And
a baby's babbling. Intermittence. Tiddle-dum-dee. And
a leaking roof. This too. Tap. And pattern : sitting down,
taking notes, time, notice, drip, play, counter it –
though graceful bits fit over "the truth"
awkwardly, don't they?
(I'll retype this). Catch. Drop.
Now baby's getting closer up corridor
more excited (this end-room full of paper
El Dorado) and I'm getting anxious
for my work/in El Dorado.
      Three things on method:
flexible, invisible, fast.   Well, hello there then.

    The wind inventing the river in the trees
    a snail glazing a trail over a stone.

Instances

For instance:

in this story this afternoon/this/all one way
these long narrow darts the angle of the wind
the angle of the window and the angle of your head once or twice
it/cut the deck/soon changes   watch
to fatter drops which after a space coalesce
trick down in shadow-parallels
as their weights and the winds dictate but for occasional
chance junction in the dance/design/whatever so that
the movement the staggered the zigzag then straight again
a tapdance then almost then sunshine again

and again
moreover
withe: willow or binding of flexible twigs
hadn't known that one

and, moreover,
the pia mater, delicate innermost
of the three meninges of the brain
and spinal cord al'uum al raqiqah, tender
a tender mother –
its function?
but that another book here just
the blithe supra-reality of words
(insert stifled)
what leave out or
and for long periods between other periods
working at it for any "reason"
concision, excision
more humility, mere humility not the first
sick facetiousness, bizarre deafness
bizarre self-confidence
Rhine Rí abhann King of Rivers
Rhône ró abhann fast river
Garônne garbh abhann rough river
Seine seach abhann separating river (think seachas: besides)
Shannon sean abhann old river
Avon   easy   itself

deep in the dark
to find there is there   something
something that   however irregularly
ruled by/what
how do you do
how do you do
fine thanks I'm
you too   me too   & you
oh.

In Paul Klee's sketch
Steamers in Port his lines are
almost everywhere but where
between shift and each quick
sidestep only the four
parti-coloured funnels
stick to their while all the other
strokes and dashes take variously
off around the as the representation
is this the point? goes on
in the blank areas between
almost beside the obvious
drums down incessant rain
while at the same time dripping vertically
even tinkling through this intimate section
of the inside of the wilder structure of a storm
from a gutter outside to a brimming barreltop
piccolo while laid over this the emphatic whack
of the wind driving the rain's dance slaps the manmade
roof by turns in waves and curves and lines and
almost-circles staying put.

It's gone.
I stretched back in my chair
arms up
day-dreaming
and that pain was gone.

A quality when sky opens
cloudless in early morning
November and your breath stays
around and this laketop's flat
and receptive to light that comes
clear through otherwise
hills melting into cloud
is that a heron?
stripped from the sky
leafless treetops in pools
in the road in the sky

A Record of Emotion

Side A

locked into themselves with their own
geometries private & for sale as if all the time
there is an echo to significance
in telling. Take any rule of thumb
& apply it. Something as disappointing as
memorable speech or mot juste/out of true/(tie the lace
& take a bow) & it will fit no doubt if a bit bumpy at
ankles elbows fit as much as matters
if, if yr sights are quite low enough.
In its telling   its way through
snagged & barbed in that tunnel of quirk
& convention & mass suspension of disbelief
is dark a pertinent exclusion from the Sermons
on Importance when you are old & grey & full of shit

immense difficulty of happiness
without equipment flexible enough to discuss that subject
stays submerged each box facing a like box
filled with glossy material for hope for the other
producing despair being
things that are equal to the same thing
being equal to each other in this one world however much
eyewash in the romance mating strategy
step foot hand dance fog
most folk being bipedal hominids
you know these days any
how do you do anyway swirl in
& focus   shadowy   fix &
swirl away

"I say, look," said Peter in amazement,
"a castle on a cloud. Who lives there?"
"I don't know," said Chinky, "I do hope
it's someone nice. I don't want to meet
a Giant this morning."

*

Yes. No. Please. Thank you. I like it.
I don't like it. That is too expensive.
Please let me have. How do I get to…?
What time is it, please? I need.
I would like. I don't speak. I don't understand you. These

are important expressions.

I'm sick of the rich
I'm sick of their insolence
I'm sick of their insolence of display
I'm sick of their effort not even to know
of the problems of the poor as they take from them
taking taking in one insistent dimension vigorously

I'm sick of being poor

heavy chestnut blossom by a shed wall by a river.
Mud & buried bicycles & reflections in the channel.
Fifty-seven seagulls on a parti-coloured roof.
Your move. Maytime.
To swink in this railway station buying time
to think, static, in kinetic railway context by the rails.
To push carry drag baggage zigzag through a crowd on a platform.
Sorry. Check. Counter-check. Re-do. Excuse me. Thanks. Sex.
Carefree the heavenly bodies of women too
in the station on the go. Good morning.
Let it be a good morning. This too. Though.
(Do it well, your death. Quietly at work in the dew).
Coming round.

5 Freedoms of Movement

Making almost no sound in here in this other room
curious turning pages quietly & taking notes
meticulous getting the (other) picture in bit by
bit & writing almost silently & yet in the next
room my baby daughter wakes as if meticulous she can
sense or dream my presence into her sleep to expel
her & cry out for a while then stop quieten stop
meanwhile into that silence that is a gap/active
to wait in cower almost from which I can attend
(corners like this) though always imagining that
refuge is/but thinking & each extension failing
to predict the silence like this now broader without
prelude sleep.

Alien clear moon in a clear sky frost
which trivial details it is so cold
yr fingers a key is turning in a lock
& a dozen keys turn simultaneously
turning static somewhere as in music
it would seem along the block.

stop. Placing a melon by the tips of his fingers he
sliced an inch depth from the top
stood it up then nipped off a
cap from the other end in the same way
exposing deep yellow flesh & paused
then brought his knife down carefully steadily
along every second external groove until
half the fruit came away
with each slice cutting off a small piece at one end. Stop.

Then he ran the knife between flesh
& rind of each separate slice
curving upwards before each end   pausing
finally gutting the central sac of seeds
carefully   in silence   very carefully. Stop.

His only other contribution for the night
was to make a sex joke in dialect Italian
imagining we wouldn't understand.
Her *il grande amore* with displeased relish
listing the dialect words for it.

Side B

To make a table
you need wood
to make the wood
you need a tree
to make the tree
you need a seed
to make the seed
you need fruit
to make the fruit
you need a flower
to make a table
you need a flower.

the colour black the colour the sheerness
the colour hostility. what these squabbling
natives lack

magari

withering

injured   as if

not perceptibly
our capacities
childhood adolescence adulthood
amazed at
what seems missing
as life "advances"
thinning into obsession

the most dogged found whimpering.
many things are a pity. pulse faster. by comparison.
the heat terrible. static shadows thicken across each
shadow. this shit. still pacing steadily in one line
towards I find. it is extraordinary even to me a little

men making reports
addenda minutes instructions
incurred deferred carried out
the hinges of civilization opening
& closing   distinctly
Civilization   civilization

you need a flower

adaptations are many. look.
like the daysleeping moth
when its restplace blackened
its camouflage inverts blatant
a famous example/exterminated/birds
thriving for a while voraciously. until.
      so that when the caterpillar
      prepares for pupation the fully
      fed ichneumon larvae bite their
      way out through its skin spin their little
      yellow cocoons all round the remains
& "personal suffering" ?
from this point of view is
      there may be a hundred or more of
      them. another small ichneumon wasp
      drives its ovipositor through the
      skin & tissues of the feeding caterpillar
      & into these tiny grubs themselves
      developing parasitically inside
      the caterpillar parasiting at times
      the parasitic grubs of its own species
baroque. & efficient too. many things
      or develop in the egg of the host
      be laid in the egg but develop in the
      larva be laid in the larva & complete
      development before or after pupation
      of the host or more rarely have all
      their development in the adult.
variety. & to escape them?
      a wood wasp larva burrowing deeply
      into a pine trunk may seem safe
      but that long ovipositor through
      solid binding slides an egg down puzzle
      the larva's vulnerable succulent flesh
stealth. confidence? the spreading terror
of one's own augmenting stupidity!
      attached to the skin or hairs of

       the victim laid on plants likely
       to be eaten by the victim hatch
       in the victim's alimentary canal
       laid in places frequented by any suitable
       victim species anywhere hatch into minute
       active larvae
hello. each hatch. bids welcome.
buzzer. until some end is. that set
face (check yr friends). hello.
       especially in their later stages
       contact with the air connect their
       rear spiracles original opening made
       in the host's body
(Shakespeare on this)
       or one of the larger tracheae &
       use the air for their own respiration

some people are dead.
it would seem. you can touch them in the street
as they pass you shopping   busy. intent.
even a breeze a breeze commits to literary cliché
its own impress in long grass in the park. as you might think.
by the railings with the chickenwire
keeping out that rubbish that blows
by the time it takes to cross the street
& lights change red & breezes turn
the waves/you can feel them. sensible creature.
you & I together have been sometimes
hands held tight the sweat in the centre
creases where those fingers that you've had for quite
some time now & since then & where they begin
not understanding there where the repetition in the tide of
retrospect getting along forward always are you hallowed
hallowing where *clamant the birds in the dawn after the party
sleep my poppet* fine *my conscience* fine thanks *memorie* fine
sleep since I've heard from you anything since
heard from getting along past you how are you since
& where've you been all this time time

in some lives. sometimes not. I don't know. not certainly.
& when it is not overlapping (you need a flower)
songs about its periphery fill the gap.
or reproduce the memory. or sharpen the desire.
which could be called ambition. which is a pity.
no. there it is, to interest us. good. a blank.
to think to discover something in the act
of obliterating it with something cruder
thin black blades of the wings of swallows
a large brain & a long childhood
leaves branches water (where was I?)
with all those ornate figurations in meta- this & that
(branches) climbing while truth dwindling in proportion
to the glare of accentuated frill will. well.
many mouths moving. no wonder nobody with any sense

to make a table
you need wood
to make the wood
you need a tree
to make the tree

neat it may be
being vibrant
& young yes
detest that squashed plane but have
stave off its though neat it
fidget around a point to be
because reasons
on these lines
I'm in no no neat
not possible
if accuracy is anything
singlemindedly aimed at
that single is wrong there
care & delight physical
call it delight is a lot
to go on
reason shaped
tapered
blurred &
bland too
you can play with it
efficiently alone a lot
slot into anywhere
where/one usually can
&/but then this
as it enters is another subject
effecting a shift
if/well textually

mounting a long narrow nose
of a saddle

tight blue sheen

bizarre habits of
the inhabitants of this place
placed repetitious
observance of token
to counter-token
beyond the ken of the more so
& did so as times eroded
ornate details
entailed in their accepted cult:
folk masses after mass voting & votive masses
for folk bored to fuck & warming to insult

      pale beach in remote zone
      to be very happy despite all
      a shell   another shell   coiled   inside which
      after which   ear to ear
      I was stopped in my tracks then by a tiny spider
      on white sand going somewhere
      lost to the lyrical scientific habit of
      indulgence of pattern   for a period
      of saying why not?   why not

making lists persistently for instance
things in the next day's sequence numbering
every night your little kaleidoscope of yes/no decisions
crossing each item out with a coloured biro
through the following daytime daily
for a laugh keeping those batteries crackling. precisely.
but nothing gets finished. & nothing goes on.
deeper in debt & richer by half transferring
deference from one day to the next I
being on the move sticking fast to catch
damned if miss a flourish when such
arrives then itching back to business
full throttle some days even making it to relish a cancel
itself to balance against your glass castle/continuing

rat a tat tat who is that?
only grandma's pussy cat.
what do you want?
a pint of milk.
where's your money?
but that's not funny.
where's your pocket?
I forgot it.
O you frivolous pussy cat.

*

to recapture details

        before yr decision

just as they were   exactly so
is not possible

        after yr decision.

it was perhaps the best thing possible
in the circumstances.

        that "now" can mean

nothing.
as I say…

cloth gathering into that point
movement of movement inside that

persistent undersound of a river. hardness.
table facing a square window inset in a deep white wall.
the four places. & more. head of a narrow angular stairs.
a bracket of brilliant green. fracture.
sometimes an animal passes. brown white black.
a fly sometimes in sunlight.
sometimes a man.

•

move.
woodslatted ceiling
where a small skylight (streak)
that remained   light
then a window giving out on a field
a section of granite drywall. glints.

•

move.
through glass: elsewhere: hillside.
some trees. one bright barn. red.
another ripple   arriving late

•

move .
four homemade watertanks to flat low roofs placed over/lustre/
long grass in a tiny yard with sunlight moving through it
to make straight lines waver
here/there   in the aorta of the city
two sparrows go by through it
with energy

•

persistent wonder-sounds in the roothairs shiver.
lustre: resinous.   *habit:* prismatic.   *hardness:* three.
fracture: splintery. *streak:* white.
  △ (fierce dog) ╪ (gypsies not liked)

thin length of wallpaper
exposed inner wall
half-demolished house
where was "upstairs" once
displaying cream yellow pink blue
of/on a wall underneath
showing through

now gone   that's it
a short torn flap
blowing to the left
disconcerts
not being in formal concert
making it in the sticky medium
of coherence the human skin

being a porous membrane
tra-la world moving through
it as if mist made of mist gone
to Standa Maurice back soon
as allwhen through ambitact

to make a bedframe creak
for a little while
in the half-light
giving your nerve-ends a good time.
flower   table   stem

5 Freedoms of Movement

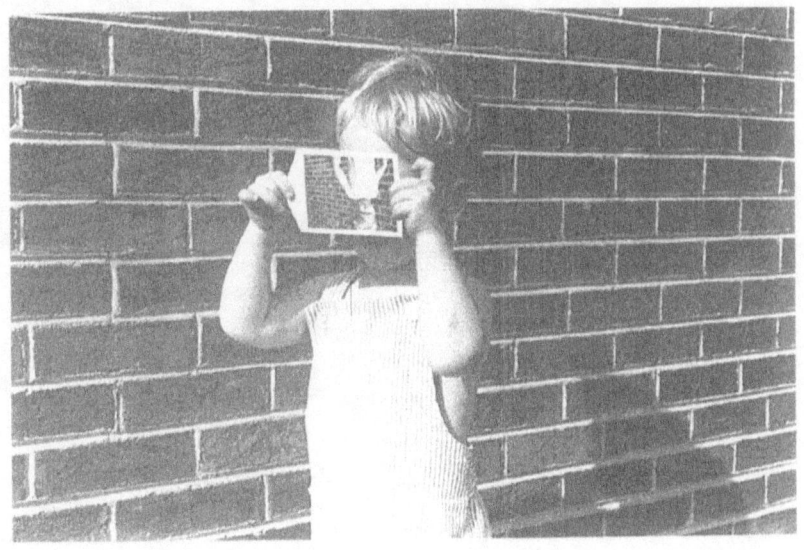

Two Caterpillars

There once were two young caterpillars, Fat Caterpillar and Fatter Caterpillar, that lived on a windowsill under a tree. Their windowsill was white and our caterpillars were white and green and they ate and ate and slept and slept quite happily on the white windowsill under the tree.

One day a bankman came to the tree with his money and sat under it balancing a book. But he soon fell asleep and began to dream. And in his dream he saw a bankman falling asleep under a tree with his money and a book and beginning to dream of a man dreaming he was making money out of a book (in which he featured quite prominently) under a tree beside a windowsill upon which were two young caterpillars, laughing, white and green, Fat Caterpillar and Fatter Caterpillar, that dreamed they lived on a windowsill under a tree.

You couldn't believe how happy they were.
You couldn't believe how fat they were.
They were very fat. And very happy.

Until one day an Autumn Leaf fell on the Fatter Caterpillar to the sinister snip of scissors and the day went black. Like that : ☞ ▬
How interesting. You can't do much under an Autumn Leaf though, so the Fatter Caterpillar, sensibly, fell asleep. And in his dream he saw

between paper & trees where sun
gets through between the branches to the grass
under a leaf on a curving stem – the pseudo-fairytale
before the "lyric"/two actors play beforehand too –
how's this? a girl goes by from elsewhere
to set street music its cryptic rhythm against another
how you can live to a different beat an old radio
in a hut on a deserted building site paid little to
live & as to writing/well! but between stations
to pick up the possible & go on with that from there

1

she paces up & down the room. lies down. turns/her love-grief
delicacy in the clammy tropical night. pretends to try to read.
who's that? pale profile in skeletal light through slats.
wind in the street playacting along with   music

2

gantries through fog enter the city from the port
take yr imagination along that track alleyways streets
where nobody not yet chill collar up the script
woodpigeons somehow wads growing with each
breath in yr breast pocket/very popular very human

tight cloth in motion
over pelvic rhythm. black.
dark the eyes too.
swept past with an eye-kiss
on the street
which they still do
in this city
despite.
which was returned
with thanks   & best wishes

this music goes like this   hollows   twists
pauses developing in places
you follow   then
wonder how it works wonder where I
or as if sideways
to right   then   leans
forward into its own   *danger*   against implications
laughing   back   on the radio/the flickering batteries
of what I have/pressed   & a bit down/well   watching/on the site
tenacious details of daily getting by
fog interspersing   as   no   some mist   emphasis
counter simultaneous emphases/bustle in enclaves underground/
& a ghost from another station

Voici ma famille
ma femme
    mon fils   ma fille
et moi.
Je suis Monsieur Legrand.
Ma femme est Madame Legrand.
Ma femme est assise.
Elle lit un livre.
Marie est debout
près de la fenêtre.
my wife the sun the rent
Je suis assis dans un fauteuil.
is due my headache is due
to your headache
Pierre est à genoux sur le plancher
il joue auec son train.
Pierre is screwing
that tart from Kimmage.
Bonjour mon ami.
Écoutez s'il vous plaît.

diverge these gaps filling with what may be
who knows look round you that blade noticed
each elsewhere the pages the books the instances
detailed may be dances to your ears as one changes
understanding if you can more music
kitten in the bidet/what did she ever say
our what really is matter to be expressed our
our bright tininess our understandings reticulated
balances go by in the street on fire they look
look at you look at them we meet they-you-I & retreat
parry & plunge & finally at the band where
waves mesh redissolve where memory &
remembered memories diverge & play over the air
as the air itself is known to play diverging

doing business.
getting your knife in deep & clean
preferably into as many as it is possible
to line up simultaneously in a good
straight voluntary & vulnerable file
(memory) then suppressing that adrenal twitch
to simplify the mind
& steady the hand (memory)
turn hard & true. through memory.
through life. a package deal one says.
to make a killing one says.
    unpredictable high velocity
    confidence in ignorance to be eaten
    hatch in the victim's alimentary canal
    laid in places frequented by any suitable
    victim species hatch into minute active larvae
    later stages Collide There are things we meet
    They have nothing to do with/Flash/Don't let it end

Credit all this lumber! Pages. Five hundred books
at least. Shelving (shaky). A desk (ditto). Typewriter.
Erasers. Tipp-Ex, blade, pens, pencils, markers, chalk,
pocket dictionaries – Italian, Spanish, Latin – a
large Webster, C.T. Onions's Concise Etymological,
Dineen's Irish Dictionary, deBhaldraithe's Irish/English,
Garzanti's Grande Dizionario (riddled with curiosities),
envelopes, copybooks, notebooks, paper clips, stapler,
box of staples, a red disintegrating address-book. The
beginning. There is more. Mug of hot coffee – to get
life moving, tissues – for approaching 'flu, wastepaper
basket, gas fire – turned off: economy in the cold,
bulging folders on which: notes outcrowding notes
aggregating towards a tentative mound: Pieces In Transit,
Odes, Hymns, Notes for Book in Process – uneasy companions,
in process. Various insects would seem to display a similar
madness of aggregation but that even a superficial study
will reveal the logic of. Peep through that ceiling.
Display a man at work! The preliminary foray of a
new entomology. Begin taking notes.

        trees leaf
        & leaves shift
        in the air
        figures & machines are passing by
        discontinuously through zigzagged strips
        of sunlight & shadow
        that enzebriate the street outside
        the street
        outside the street
        & it strikes me
glasses   plates   dishes   stray spoons
disorder diminishing   hands warm   racks   shelves
appointed places   transitoriness in the stormship
a blurred recurrent light in mist.
my daughter playing. quaint notion of permanence!
successive stabbings at the brain-place
peer through a powerful lens beam in
(toothache/earache) everybody home? *si, certo, si*
        open yr head & gather it all in
        detailing the names faces circles
        railway stations squares a park
        the single rooms circles trees
        stains on a wall sunlight on
        a wall sunlight through leaves &
        branches sunlight on water moving & still
        sunlight somebody combing her hair somebody
        singing whistling watching herself shadows
        rooms places windows names rooms doors
                the release is so fine sometimes
                sometimes   sudden self-anger
                sometimes   blank falling
                I forget the most simple things elsewhere
                wherever my mind elsewhere taking a walk as if
                among very many as if's very
                demanding labyrinthine but I think I
                think lost

odd you know   I still meet them in the street
& there seems a new solid film over their features
the mobility calculated now
not quick now with energy   inner/older   masked
I read too much into it or
well   shifty
they're half thinking the same thing
too   *him!*

(As to our bankman who'd fallen asleep balancing a book under a tree beside the windowsill upon which resided our fat, happy and rather clever caterpillars, Fat Caterpillar and Fatter Caterpillar, he woke up when the river – which we forgot to mention – over-ran its banks, and drowned.

And all the fish caught all the money.

Of course it was a great and terrible outrage and the nation mourned. Even Fat Caterpillar and Fatter Caterpillar who'd suffered a change of heart and outlook paused for a moment in the sunlight – two very bright and beautiful butterflies – as a mark of respect to his memory on some tulips on the coffin. Before moving on).

One Wallflower

patterns green after rain bright
tap in spaces between where each
leaf is different to each different
trees root carrying each array of
difference to the others/constituents
which reoccur made of ivy nettle lilac
to a beat sycamore//more or over or under
which each individual eye & its capacity to
aggregate overwhelmed easily individually
for breathing to breathe in each experiment
at last fast but to/lasting

at the chair
at the mirror
at the wall
at the door
at the sky
at the glass
at the border
at the second-on-the-left
at the blue & grey sign
at the tip of the bay
at the handle
at the floor
at the rug (mind)
at the key (click: fits)
at the knob
at the wall
O: at yr window: look
that a life may consist
a complicated
elaborate
& deliberate
detour   odd

walls red to waist level
cream the rest of the way up
ceiling cream & fading
the room small
walls high
& on the one opposite
three framed photographs of bits of
Ireland in black & white.
a red formica-topped table
in the centre of the room
& rows of red chairs around the walls
& hare krishna penned in small neat cursives
on a cream surface beside the door. bow.
the voice behind that door is bored.
now it is speaking on the phone.
now it speaks to an applicant in the room.
one can judge. one is free. to interpret anywhichway.
recall. or (hear it) that to speak or pause be a trap.
apt. pat. a compact. bow down. down. look up. welcome.
now: the procedure is this.
now it is you. won. one. un. om. turn. & now:

arrive at a mirror
(I've spotted red rimming the silver)
  walk: stop: talk: stop:
  talk: balk: (at that)
  balk: stop: walk again
away
(with)
silver pots
in yr articulate hand

  deep luminous each blade each point
  each way through/down, at play, grips:
  you need a place, a home, a ground, you need
  not need, inured to it, Need; that.
  if/though who am I to hear here to say
  hearing more birdsong in that other language
  (not in this book) I could/but/then flower,
  seed-bobbin, a leaf in a stream

  (still)

it is most important to hold
steady. this especially applies
to making sure the subject
doesn't doesn't move move suddenly
& & don't stand too close

  still

still to take care not to load or unload
in strong sunlight & make sure the
side/back is closed properly & tight
so that no light
can leak through

this to keep open to feed in "knowledge"
to keep/until bounds break:

the first child

you will now
concentrate
on the file: life
e.g. : egg.
one centre at
which sense ensues
sus: fly: nervure & thorax:

or anxious to veer near
the centre applause
to ape you-me-us
tap on the drum here please
finger & thumb   to fact
clarifact
until it too has a son
& too progeny
& the progeny progeny

quite another thing in sunlight
under multiple leafpattern cording & limber
to be lyrical
in the open where the guns are

for argument you need words
in blocks fit to ideas with
sticky ends to fit block for
block together. *It.* sometimes
through a distance (here
sleepeth Eliza Bodkin, departed
this Lyfe) they lose their fray
wear sometimes one idea destroys
the rest about it bare before
without making more possible
immediately.

it is a vulnerable period for
any carrier of such an idea.
power to work against the bearer.
arcane places maybe. only so.
for a time. wary to develop
other pieces pictures at
corners of which are
clusters of venomous conclusions.
you should see where this got
me. O baby. but then
vulnerability carries you to
the defence on a stretcher
among thickets. glorious. though
defence is m' m not a discussion
& the argument

I'll tell you
I'll tell you
said a teller
something was going on
above his head again
wait

we did
we did wait
we waited

realizing variants
are it in the dark
around which out of from through

it's lovely   thank you
brief & precise description
of a thing by its properties
lost in a forest of shifting synonyms
a crime compounded by making of ideas
& of things an array of coiling
in the mist in the forest from the ground
up a shape in fog the fog a shape
mist in a forest: in place of respect
for/love of/delight in/only instead that
tacky cement of *as if*

some blown dust catches
in a crevice in the concrete by the gate
moistens it rains blows then more
dust. earth compacting daily & so until
a seed & rain & a little more humus & then & then
& a
a hairlet & rootlet grasping growing
life that unlocks a pattern
that mimics a fight
to be discovered each phase
until this surprising late phase
a flower incongruous in concrete by a gate
where dogs piss   marking off a mate
or a place where/a wallflower
& a sweetish whiff

it is an *occasion* in that sense too
that I knew it: that quite particular colour
dark but clear & the cool smell of rain on
a changed breeze
meaning rain
looking up from where my
nose was leading through
a tight schedule
allows relief   elsewhere
more air in lungs & cooler
a white line in a blue sky
moving & the mind   laughing at itself

Livelihood

for Mary

prelude

THE PILLAR & THE VINE

Rest
   happiness
      peace

why is the white so
difficult touched
suddenly

a tendril travelling
& a leaf with it
hacks at

a pillar a gate the
facts chips at
plashes the

pillar at the front of
a house a huddle
in rocks

the pillar the vine
its soft white
stone

wandering beyond the puny
into the light net
this pillar

this vine hard to in shadows
discard patterns that
smash their way

into yr face anyway to let go
the lattice & as you've
seen it just as & in

a flash you've noticed/frequency
times length/then smile
dropping ripples

onto a watersurface
where
tiny

    eggs

fell
      lightly

moving

    in the

wind

     around the

edge of the

  base of the

  stopped

stone pillar beside
where to keep
putting

betterparts together
under pressure
against

Despair/rest
happiness/
then

(peace) in an access
of wisdom
sit

down shut up
the pillar
takes

the wind (times length)
whatever it was that
was possible to

be true to this difficulty
where fl = v & v
is velocity

the light in the heat
& the Light Apart
from all

that too a fly on a page
lands & disappears
a good ten

years on yes (times length)
(good) the pillar the
vine

arched at a black dog
brown dog/in full/
the pillarvine

hacks this pliant
this pliancy
this young

vineplant attached
to the rocky
edges

      of the pillar
      & in a rain
      of names

      absorbency

      storyline

                  two-way

    three-way

         in section

                      vertical

cut across &

      down

      rest/pillar/
      shock – curl –
      happiness

      peace/the pillar
      the vine the
      soft

      white the pillar
      the soft the
      light

      vine then just
      don't think
      don't

      look don't
      brea-
      the.

STONE

Suddenness of
the end of
things

of that end of things
freaked with jet
as if

a penpoint purred
then
it

did & thunder thundered:
NOTHING! at the
gate

[Hans Arp laughs]
(|) vast in
vast (|)

in this truly vast
si(chip)lence
in the

mass(|)ve far & dis-
persal into the
(mesh of

(|) patter + n =   )
has gone to the
edge of need

has opened a book
///has closed it
not I can tell

you things I can tell
you this littleness
this door opened

or at least it swung
on its hinges if
that's not

quite the same reversal
of the next thing
which *take us*

home pleaded the dice
inside tight on
the floor

& whingeing which I
did against a
slight

wobble in the chak-
ra & my better
judgement –

amethyst – ruby –
small chipped
(/) script

(padded envelopes
 to padded cells)
& a

few clichéd remarks
about memory & love
(eyes)(go down)

weedkiller + the
withering dry
what-not

of the plot (& across)
(reading) I who
could never

read you of a sudden
reading yr
stone

reading yr
  stone.

Take one, turn two, tack
two, catch. Five. First bit.
Then switch over, jump.
Hop twice, pitch twice, catch
one, shout. End of second bit.
Turn Death. Under the Circle of Life.
It's a long trek.
With a hoop.

Hammer tapping the root of the place
sick of the slick weary of theory
ball peen cross peen mark & trace
the Glass Slipper & the Tooth Fairy.

the basic colours

a watchman's log

How many kinds of colour have you?
Have you the basic colours?

– English/Greek phrasebook

I think yes
I was touring the lattice
now that all the little cars were grey
ah yes he said she said
    hey they said I'm
    we've got a new book out
    have you seen it
    they said
    quick! bus red
    notebooks in your
    pockets I it's about
it I think they
said it's about
    disparate/desperate
battles of a lifetime
(love, death & the rentman)
    fading/phasing
I could barely with great care
hear then
just the lips & in the eyes
that aggressive glare.
    Elsewhere: peace
    bric-à-brac
    pieces
    the night – the rain –
    the mistakes I make
    the delight to find in them
    interstices
    & to make that too a delight
    all that
    to listen
    to look
    to you or else
    one-two
where ash trees' leaves go
back & forth in the breeze
then stop
    then show back again
undergreen silver over shadowgreen

under light bright new leaves
on top
waving
> *tap*
> *I was talking to you were*
> *saying*
> *our minds…*
> *the dance*
> *the cars had once been blue in the dust.*

Books & non-books.
Poetry (space) "is an activity
not a body of reading."
> *I wonder how the Gem School feels about that?*

Click beetle or skipjack
everything wrapped up snug
in the importance of its own name
in a copybook
> *but when things get done*
> *without prattle people prattle*
> *we did it.*

Invisible bedtrap
āttōrcōppe
illusion of a whisper
brushed off.
> *Then … Robert Frost on a motorbike*
> *in the snow hearing a sinister swish*
> *of conspiracy on the fire-escape*
> *growls*
> *you cruel*
> *heart-carrier I*
> *feel myself about to*
> *until a burst of the best possible*
> *otherwords out of the blue*
> *changes everything*
> > *(spider: weaver)*
> *you were saying?*

The wine farting in its jar.

on site: A

sonnet/There is a grey sky.
    there is a white gull
    on a black aerial
    on a black roof
    opening its yellow beak
    wide & silently
    calling calls.
    snow on a street
    underneath. look out
    that window
    follow the sentence
    of a single set
    of footprints
    marking a dance
    away somewhere

    of
    someone lightly going
    silently through
    chill air
    & not calling
    not calling back:
    dawn.

    two shadows
    a third
    grey ply
    black
    flash by.

sonnet/neon flecks join & pass
    on black water
                    gull
                    teal
  but ons in speciall in thyn arraye
I see well
it passes
      clamp
two luminous blanks   rainbow splotch
OK Hey Johnny! Johnny!
JOHNNY!   Fuck you
          are fluid
          & hooded or stitched so as
white in twilight   carved scowls midarch
& close up
the Little Barrel's sexy sketches in thin array
              gullwing
              head flicking
                    claw in glove
though all curve & flow
stiletto clack   HEY   tap
seam of the knickers showing through
                  then not
engage the array of the discarded on the streets to live
singing: *& shake them from the fist*
      & let them flie
pools   blood   starlings that settle

              nets
              in flight
              in half-light
              quite
              again quick
              join
              never "to be absorbed"
              again & pass
              join & pass

              gone.

sonnet/when our landlord asked what
    I a teacher
    he'll get his rent anyway
    both knew
    if just keep out of each other's
    way. eyes.

          did. shook hands.
          a good year.
          scribbling
          drafty annex

working as a
teacher
porter
watchman
noteman
manman
changing ply for
changing   chance
working at
just ahead of the posse

        this & that ylang ylang

sensitive tips of the fingers/yr care
meditative tips of the fingers/yr care
dreaming feeling along rapidly sensitively
supple smoothnesses blank spaces tentatively
forming conjectures to be very careful to be
full of ways to begin they're still here

        as if the violin
        were not also a machine

    toyclouds on toyblue in

        toyland

sonnet/listen:
    list those bullies
    & their wishes.

    moves I needed to remember on
    site oh just give us yr money
    I needed to remember

    hooks
    on a nearby population
    /*bang*/orange plastic pince-nez

    I needed to remember
    just give us the money
    orange plastiscrap of cheese on a
    no orangepeel step.
    surely you see that. (Brecht)
    the money. checkered.

    there
    between chimneys
    in th'eye of the net
    couchant on sable
    pebbledash flak'd to where
    yr move
    listen
    old yellow underbrick pock'd & porous
    a magnificent spider

        (one brick two
        catch me
        three)

    staving off all aggressive
    parasites. the money.
    let's talk about this.
    the police are superfluous
      "even people fight
        not just kids"

tin parachutes
golden parachutes
that's real!   that's good!
to have invented
happiness. sit down. stand back.

lip service moving intricately
unmoving the eyes dead –
touch a web/send a message.

glass panels slide open stop
"yes?" cut. & you have no
possessions. collections of
(care. contact.)

but

massive malicious technoplay
click clack   /click/
as: "twirling the edge"
the dye set
underlight/overdark
as – speak:
etymology's idiotic hobgoblins
watch   wait

    two textures (at peace)
    a third (encroaching)
/*bang*/   Imix   Ik   Akbal
      Kan

sonnet/a way peachtree branches arc
loaded at the tip. I will please you
with pattern & no one will read you
no one will read you until you've been
chopped & laundered. no one. if this
worries you. someone will attempt
taking the money if someone thinks
they will read you. it's 4.02. dove-
coo & a toilet tank filling & a cock
crowing: nobody could not say it's not
music, picking up the pattern by which
to please the process receptors. then I
said. then a choir, I could hear it
through doors, windows, fly-mesh,
burglar bars, walls, tin roof,
the pageplace – each filter in quiver – a
choir, a magnificent hosanna, ooo ha-ha-ha
a-appy day! blooming, spread.

sonnet/wigs stiff with grease, white mercury,
  rouge, mice, misery – I can't stand it!
  I must. cave painting is not art/later
  that sickness. history: a grammar. make
  the present perfect – leave it!

  mentally nodding, shaking yr head, wanting
  out, out of here, most of the time, voting
  for Inside when Outside counted the cards,
  a blundering puppet locked into this template,
  an idiot, a stupid … a fool, a blithering
  thick, I…

  …I have nothing to say about that.

  watching the hand in the pocket
  move making the folds move
  watching the folds of the pocket
  move imagining that hand imagining
  movement of its fingers & wrist
  deftness under/over yr conversation
  with my conversation   you were saying?

  tin roof + rain = tinroof rainmusic.
  look at that & tell me what you see.

 peaches whose fur   sweet fruit smell
    curved groove   three senses
           then taste one

The Basic Colours **123**

sonnet/(we went out to look at a tree.
    we formed a circle around it.
    this is the Bole, these the Branches, that the Canopy –
    stand back. underneath you know
    is where the Roots go
    to live & hold the Ground together.
    & look at its Top
    how compliant it is to the weather.

    breezes intervene between leaves & us
    & tilt the shapes of themselves for literate
    old Yahoos like us to note
    & have sophisticated doubts about.
    now this is very fine!
    this will cover yr cracked earth in clover
    this will keep you out of the mines
    believe me, forever.
    hands, arms, hearts,
    organize & activate,
    their lists barbed black about
    our multicoloured tree
    soughing quietly under everything
    believe in me – believe in me –

    it breaks up in
    to pieces the
    truth
    did you
    know that
) the yellow castle   ) terrace of life
) the germinal vesicle
) the
    I see nodded each student in this dance
    intent, pretending, chipping at the fact
    to teach me something, something quite different
    I see   I think).

sonnet/you were saying? that was
precisely. a clue. dis-
carded invention. our problem
was how the question was the
more I thought I knew the more I
"knew" I sank into those relative
shadows that seem to cover the a-
symmetrical skin that one begins
to suspect anyway covers everything.
full of. everything differently
precisely in each different net.
full of tiny bright word*ks* of
discorded invention. our lives,
glittering, reticulated. & from in
here that edge where what you've
been taught to imagine you know
meets more: quote cut quote & in
this dream of learning (a fish, a
frond, a ball, a calabash) the panel
twists, splintering: "I think I
let me see I *think* I wait I mean I…"

but to continue our little chat/*tangled print*
(a fossil) once thought to be the tracks
left by a worm now thought to be either some
excrement of some fish or the stomach of a/stencilled
on the backs of buses crammed with baggage
& passengers, weaving across desolate
mountains – kids' angular dances in the dust,
conical hills, stone outcrops – diving full-tilt
to the plains, through clouds of red dust, black
smoke, in shimmering white script, ghostly:

    CONSTRUCTED BY
   /clouding, clearing, clouding/
    UNITED BODIES

  Tebang

sonnet/Dear X,

    I would like to clarify a few points:

    i) the libretto's improbable, sure.

    ii) that Irish saying is, I think: *Ní féasta go rósta; ní céasadh go pósadh.*

    iii) No, yr money order did not arrive.

    Many thanks for yr interest in my work.

    Yours etc

sonnet/fell, sick with pain on the track.
       that's a sweatdrop; this is a battle;
       succulents orchids heat & *ack ack cha*
       deep in the undergrowth. this is a cliff-
       top hidden by trees that rise to the lip
       of the rock where/stand back! listen/
       pick up that whisperpounding of the sea
       in this this is yr own pulsebeat faster
       than. "inside out" flowers. gigantic flowers.
       flowers that loom & prod, yellow & violet
       & blue & women that come by heads laden
       (verb?) & a child, sweatless. this is a
       track ascending. skyglimpse. *ack ack.* I
       think. gone. this is *cha* this is *ack ack*
       ack this is a guineafowl checking with a
       what's that? slice the creeper back & a
       yellow & green spider bunched up *tight*
       in a flower.

sonnet/reach for your spray paint: that was
   precisely. a clue. those images were
   a last layer, the layers cracked &
   dried. or/let me see. that box was
   made of glass mainly. watching graph-
   paper slowly emerge from where two worlds
   hit as such, let me show you, a hybrid, a
   raw image, emerging from an instrument,
   fascinated by this fragile film, awe-struck,
   rooted to the spot etc. saying? they murder
   you in the mountains, they beat you in the
   foothills, in the lowlands, beware: quite
   an endearing little African kingdom: *I* have
   (precisely) what *you* need. each roll of
   thunder spreads & fissures, each a different
   similar drama-carpet in the dark. syn. copating
   flashes. dauntingly stolid I thought I'd...
   quick. I see. look at that & tell me what you
   see. inside there are some beautiful verbs;
   outside there is the outside. peering over yr
   fence at the outside one evening a gigantic
   mosquito swerved past my head & crashed into a
   tree. the tree shuddered & a large branch
   cracked off. just missed the dog. the cat
   froze. the mosquito stood elegant & terrible
   on her high legs. its proboscis could kill a man.
   what is the name of the noise of the rain?

...your cat catches lizards
in the heat wallstuck gliding edgy
tails torsos she
eats no chews
& spits out on our doorstep for us.
this is the language I use.
how do you like that?

.

       instance: negotiating a sea of tubular chairs
       in the piazza the elderly poet, becalmed,
       "...these are the kinds of dreams I have."
grain of the wood
grain of the wave
       instance: the line of yellowgreen diamonds
       down back & tail, appearing, stockstill,

    disappearing.

So
let
me

touch this cup
letting its hot liquid
picture (This Side Up)
tremble – slide –
reassemble

into part of me you
noticed looking into it
so. Sit – love's
undercurrent – to watch how
shadows catch now
& then multiple spines
of books that seem to
/ack-ack-ack/ in a
tide of

material life wrested or
rested yr face
creased into an abstracted
smile – meditative – relaxed –
in a room – against
sad dented
shapes one's
days take on the whole –
a collision
a trace –

crazy to
know why tides go
& how under pressure
of lies/mistakes/flow where

how such a tug is
nightly daily nightly
& daily beyond us

anyway.

Write to me soon.

on site: B

sonnet/ *Open, wondering…*

& so these little flowers
bunched up &
spoke to me & this
is what they said

how are yr friends
they said
are they all dead
they said
we heard they were
you know & feared…

a scribble of figures
inside my bursting head
opened rapaciously
to bind the rigours
of breathing suffered
(they said?) graciously
down

down they said
where little flowers go
to bed to die like us
beautiful but capricious
they hissed

bunching their parts tightly
for the dark not probed
for nectar – not likely –
not these ones not tonight
not taken not kissed

grimace & close it.
or open elsewhere:

one

toilet bucket in a lean-to shed.
cobweb in the door.
relax & watch wheatfields flow
past you here pussy willow
& weeping willow by the river
& an ashtree's rippling on a wind's fluid
influence over where we live & what we do
if that's coherent – I don't know.

I'd like to thank you for the loan of yr house.
crisp vertical layers. it's late. you're gone.
the stairs angled up to yr study, a small square
window inset low in the wall opposite yr table
my table (thanks) & the fly I'm sure we shared
through the hush of that part of the house –

(two)

flies on too through elsewhere
echo on echo (a pigeon's wings clap)
lightly taking in all the work we do
& have done & the meaning it leaves on the air
in trees, birds' bodies, bark, windows, grass –

a still stark old stone place probably
empty & broken as (pentip feeling along
pagetop) I write now – yellow dust in the sun –

& surrounded – red dust in the sun –
by (sound of a river gone underground)

by nothing at all damn it
replace this too
irritably on its shelf

stoppered.

but surely something?

cooped energies
drink in that fire at least
varieties of earnestness, stupidities...

    is this it again?

    is this it again
    gain play a
    ke ha-ha
    kereke I build a
    this split aha
    this rippling

    beat it's a beat
    that's what it is.
    made of
    what is it made of
    the Mission cuts in deep
    but the people jeer
    this beat this singular this
    I stopped everything
    the people jeer
    just to pick up
    it's wonderful
    these downtrodden people jeer
    catch it precisely
    not bend it smooth it out
    into Literature or Song or Art or
    just once in a while
    lifting yr nose from the pile

fine, but

flick the pages...

    & that was that.

    it was a small square house
    in a small square in the centre

of the city. at 1.10 a.m. most nights
an old neighbour came out of his old house
& tapped on the window of his old neighbour's
house & asked the time: *one o'clock Paddy*
go back to sleep.
& he did.
always.

& when snow came quiet came with it &
intersected at right angles to the overactive
city   motive colour

& that was that.

sonnet/flying past this
impossibly repeating lattice
occasionally touching ground,
grazing it, getting grazes from it,
at points of poignancy, tact,
a book if you can afford it
is a fat paper object
& it can open anywhere.

to return the delicious tact
of things intact: white, pliant
spine tapering to the top,
curved parallel hairs,
colours as to each whim on the planet
this part of a, this so supple,
this one peacock feather;
& a book, if you can afford it too
is a fat paper object that can
open anywhere…

buacaire: tap, had "forgotten" that.
site. *where to?* said a voice then
the voice went away, by which (as if)
time, in a sea a dark mood,
over the rocks, where there are
no rocks finishes you. (curious how
aggression's our brightest button
on the panel.) flick the pages. wind
in the figleaves, wind in the
vinefrond. a book too, if you can
afford it, is a fat paper object…

to begin
to practise planting your life
back into the picture again
flying past this
impossibly repeating malice
(whose is it anyway
& where on earth am I?)…

while things begin to dance in a ring
while things began to dance in a ring
& this thing, these things that I touch

reach out to touch me
& sting,
big garden, stand back, one wind at a time…

   she sleeps

   watch her fingers
   her long fingers

   her fingers minding unbinding
   movingly intricately
   unmoving winding
   so many/in the veins
   (folding)/years

   already

   ready

      there

sonnet/there is a grey sky.
there is a white gull
on a black aerial
on a black roof
opening its yellow
beak wide & silently
calling
calls.
snow in that
place down there
marked a street
on a map.
look out a window.
follow the sentence
of a single set
of footprints
tracing a
dance away somewhere

of
someone lightly going
silently through
chill air
& not calling
not calling back.
dawn
     /////
         gnawed all in not
but silently through
calling not air chill
going lightly someone
calling dawn-calls in
(/)dancing an aerial ring(/)
             called dawn

ah whoom! goes the orchestra. leave your
quotes by the door please, which they did,
nice sheep. then into "maturity" (ripple)
each day drowns me in a tide of sexual
memories. waiting for yr train to arrive
wavering in heat-haze, due, crashes on
through the other end of the station. is
just how the world begins. come in. an
exciting science of slicing clutter from
your life can be … I call it *poetry*.
& you? well, let's work together!

ship-ship-ship something pixel ship picked
up printout in dream & managed rictus, taptap,
knowing we all knew we were dreaming this. I
think I was regretting I wasn't taking notes.
then startling sunlight on long Georgian
windows in a square in Dublin with Schrödinger
many times gliding by – "yes, splendid, it's
a quarter past…" – aethereal cirrus on
gorgeously faulted glass.

muddling through Paradise – every small move,
agility of the hands, all the motile, useful
bits of the body – humming my own sweet tune
when, stopped short, caught in a trough, I felt –
of a sudden – cold & nauseous, opposite number
I think number 70 from under whose door a viscid
goo was definitely oozing: old frizzante (or dog-
piss?) & purple vomit. Art, Wine, Committees &
Involuntary Spasms. let's – I thought – surely
we can discuss this one.

care. contact. each frail.
act. intact. each. that's not money!
a life an array of related mistakes.
gainsea. frail joke. cat. pale zoo.
fact. each guest. tact. each risk. two
six. tat. each venge used. each look.
bract. down by the factory. into &
out of. shook. each life. verifact.
gain. every quip & nook. strain. each
vent. dent. entry. care, kiss, bend
with the wind is the 2nd Law of Thermosurvival…

Life ... life considered as a chain of
ineradicable dawn horrors.

Life as a diagram: a terminal spinney of
ampersands.

as a proscription of foreknowledge edging
forward, forward dangerously linking reality
(impossibly!) to observation.

pattern-ache vanishing into life's pixels –
your spaceship, your glider, your beehive,
your honey farm, that vast object in the dark
sky, tail spark, belly spark.

in a dense corrugation of memories (shadow/
light) + (shadow/light) making fake lacquer-work
for the books.

Life's blood   Life & death   Friends for life
Lively   Livelihood   Liver   Getting life
Getting on with yr life   Putting life back
into it   Taking over yr life   Taking yr own life
The lives of others   A lifetime away   Yr
hands   Pleading   Is that it?

as(misery)the absence a(tempting)pain attempting
to(a)drift in the contemplation of misery & pain

(Minutes of the Last Discussion)

there it is! their stealthy fiddling in the
locks, eyes level at the hide: I bide, I bide.
fix that to your crucifix & carry it!

never again. they know exactly I mean exactly
every absolutely every nothing. noise of
the voice of the seepage is to be told in bold
capitals & I, well … plaiting ripple-water
in narrow stream plus sun. and its smallwater
song, *koro koro*. in a burst of self-knowledge
I opened the beginning up through the shimmer
of the deep to find a happiness probable at
root – as opposed to this driving gully of a life.

> *[what about their eggs?*
> *how can I deal with them?*
> *I'll tell you. tell you. don't listen.*
> *listen. they've got no teeth.*
> *contrary to popular belief.*
> *however grubby the members*
> *of their families.*
> *inhabitants of the controltowers*
> *controltowers along the walls*
> *the walls around you surround you*
> *brick by what else should I do?*
> *who'll tell they check yr family?*
> *if you suspect old hats etc treat*
> *all of Eurasia let heads of state*
> *know there's been an outbreak.*
> *there's been an outbreak.]*

item: map & plan. eyes that have calm
hands that hold peace – bless & share.

but it doesn't end there. my Dearest Raging
Bull. Yrs Never Again *ka marao*. that "so much
of an artist's life can be spent in defeat"
I remember, nodding & walk on. and woke up.

they keep shaking my hands these people, demented, while I keep trying to work out which language to choose to respond to them in. not very long after this I find a dog-eared postcard in my pocket:
 "Anti-rational emotionalism lives on."

A tree beside some water's
standing still
the water there is standing
too or seeming to though full of
little dark & darting things
& fluctuant. the bird is in the tree
the wind its briefly on a branch
beside a leaf I see
twice then flies back over the ranch
to the cliff.

   o

the farmer is walking across the dust of the ranch.
ridged bootmarks in the dust of the ranch.
the sky of this place is blue. & justly famous.
one two. an envelope of useful chemical reactions.
cut down too on your tobacco intake. one four.
reaches the landrover. Tree. Stream. Bird. Cliff.

   o

the water moving by in the stream here
has many fine characteristics. look.
a bird reaches a cliff.
fenugreek folding its leaves
around its wedge-flower. Lebanese?
sundown.

   o

moonlight.

living in a world where
things happen

someone will play the viola
someone will
& someone will &

counting on it

a large crimson spider
a small silver gimmick

tearshaped appleseed
moist   mahogany

one two four
one two four three

o

presence & pressure of space one's future
boundless periods of stillness curling gradually
so that each dream congruent into the next
continuing solo in the shadows under the leaves
out of the sun in Sleepy Hollow

o

intricate mist
building on the windowpane

four kittens lap milk
from a tray on the ground.
four apples in a row
on a windowsill.

"arithmetic" (Plato)
"has a very ... elevating effect..."

(HISTORY)

      b
      a
      l
      a
      n
      c
      i
      n
      g
        on its
    quixotic
        footnotes
            wobbling
      finely
       &
       .

or the wearing repetition of children

towards you

or for a long time

crushing vividness

or

o

or
certainly fevered delusion
but
look – my health's been bad these weeks
& again, yes!
this reptilian slyness
for instance in press photos
or:
in itself   nothing
but
or:
sliding down the middle of a well-greased chute
or:
punctures the limits of mere

steel grey   grey sky

taps the sunlit circles &
hits the glass arrows clicks slaps incised
& illuminates blues & golds & a 1,000 flowers &
travels through   cleats, veins, frets
combine & mingle   brittle, crazie

cool in here

nel duomo

& for the tourist
"history"
200 lire

o

& then   she suggested this way
we won't do that again   she said   one-two

wobbling finely   the mirror tilted   so that
that something lodges   obdurately (in the net)
tilted   cool in here   in history

or.

"but how can you write about emotion
when you forget everything the next day."

/the Police are perfect.
God is perfect.
God is the Police/

    and in a cabin on a building site
    watching. hatching near spring
    to net that one pet fly.

    thrums the web to lull her
    then motions as to bind her
    (blue whale's residual pelvis)
    and rarely gets away.

/the Rule is No.
the Rule is Good.
take take take take take/
                      the pieces

pieces
now that I understand for the moment
crowded eggpouches in a crevice
by a corner of a windowpane
maybe I think I do maybe/
the little luminous pieces of the love story…

*And then I woke up. I was at a table in a
small shed on a building site in Dublin. It
was 1983 and I'd just written the words: "Site
normal. Nothing to report" in the logbook.
Nearly five, time to use the phone again. Duck
and dive. Only a newspaper spread out before me
on the table made a paper-sound and I seemed to
be full of a dream of reading, a sort of noise
in itself, I know, inside one's self ... Anyway
that's how I remember it. Don't use the phone;
not yet. I think I said a word aloud to myself
to check, to punctuate, to be certain – "certain",
the very idea made me smile! Doubtfully I turned
to scan carefully everything I was to report nothing
on and it seemed to me – at the beginning all over
again – that I might still be, maybe ... dreaming?*

*The car had once been blue
and the lorry had been brown.
The milk-van had been
bright yellow
and the bus
red.
The racer had been green
and the butcher's van
a brilliant
orange.*

*Now all
those
little
cars
were grey
without a single bit
of their bright
colours*

left (Enid
Blyton,
The Six Little Motor Cars).

zulu dynamite

the notebooks

*Voilà. The rock shattered.
Zulu dynamite, they called it.*

– *Msinga*, Rian Malan

*the pale
blue jotter*

LOG

on site

It was one of my duties as a night watchman on the site to check the site every hour on the hour & to enter in the site logbook, every hour on the hour, *Site normal. Nothing to report* then to phone HQ to report that there was, in truth, nothing to report.

Item: map & plan. *Item:* follow
the flowline in its construction
the crane makes extending piece-
meal day by day up around itself
jet, plackets, butterfly diagrams,
the steelribbed holes
in the floors, floor by
folded, flooded/one *could*
exit he thought (say) that is
arrive that is leave &
return that is travel (as a condition)
that is effect changes that is
in that box, grid, pigeonhole
getting nowhere, to scale. *Item...*
& the site watchman loses his job.

    Scaled down diffident
coiled in/in a strange way around difference
leaving itself a forgetting at the same time
doling the pieces
    the glass
    the steelribbed holes
in the floors still to the end extend until it itself

  falls still

  & is
  taken
  away &
  gaps
  are
  connected
  & cemented
& the building is trimmed, finished & inhabited:
      base
      frontage
      dome
      & sky.

:
:
:
:
:
:
:
:
:
:
:
:
:

:
:

:
:
:
:

          double choker
            soft eye
          basket hitch
           the single
            reaving
            halshing
          the cradle
the double wrap basket hitch
       & bridle hitches
              two
             three
         & four leg
for effectiveness, safety.

To write: He is sitting at his desk.
His children are sleeping. It is a
winter's evening in Ireland. He is reading.
He is working. He is about six feet tall.
He has a habit of pouting his mouth when
he concentrates. Like this. Click.

Africa, colour-loneliness, to be lonely
for *colour,* does anybody know about…?
He is 38. He has 2 children. He is poor,
yes, in a way. Detach. The rent is due.
He wears boots. A cotton shirt. The rent
is you. Twist your lens & you get to see
the albumen in the tube so that you come
up quite close to intricacy too two,
three & four legged with end-wings just
here, & here, you see?

. . .

When the sun gets up
I get up & go out.
Cat licks a forepaw
on the wall, scratches
its supple outstretched neck
with a rapid left backpaw
shakes head, & vanishes.
I fill my bucket right up.
It almost overflows
hearing that music
seeing the very
black & white of the
inside of my notebooks.

LOG

a round (& recited as a round)

Daisy
& dandelion had begun to bloom
& bent down
& picked them
& looked at the day's eye
the sun
the *dent de lyon*
garish & blunt
world vigorous & explicit
seven teeth
tipping each brilliant petal
& was greatly pleased
to be alive
& to continue to be.

Flysong
birdsong cloud-movement leafshape
white gables among trees
shimmer of heat over glass
sectioned hills
(but was I awake?)
a road catching bright dots
that glide between hedgerows
& – suddenly –
(colours of the crops)
he found himself
to his surprise still young
& daisy & dandelion had begun to bloom
& bent down & picked them &
looked at the day's eye
the sun
dent de lyon
garish & blunt
world vigorous & explicit

& bent down
to pick

vomiting blossoms
compact, propagative, unstoppable devices
that emerge, grow, bloom, close,
recede, seed, die, emerge, eager, repeating,
eating the sky's light
sick with the idea of fecundity
quick he reaches quick
clutching at rubberoid stems
that make a pert fart aghast…
everything white, green,
yellow, pink, up from Sleepy Hollow,
pallid, demented, spry, rootless, calculative,
each brilliant argument won

each poison inserted expertly
into the Politics of Enquiry
each articulation snapping into place
sapping the foundation
shot in his living-room
shot on his doorstep
in front of his wife
in front of his children
hooded & shot
abducted & shot
& no consolation in any philosophy
but one more definitive step –
deracinate, calculative –
into the stupid,
the hopeless.

Daisy
& dandelion had begun to bloom
& bent down
& picked them
& looked at the day's eye

the sun
the root, the stem,
the blaze, the perianth
trapping each tart beat of the blood
guttate, garish, blunt,
world vigorous & explicit
(spatulate/cordate
 acuminate/ovate
 pinnate/palmate)
a conduit to a pool
of dazzling illusions
with every semblance
to continue to be
(& was greatly pleased
 to be alive)
to continue to be
just that

in all likelihood.

the black notebook

LOG

local colours

What
is the name
of the noise of
the train clack-at-a-clack
& where is it going?
The god of the
noise of
the
train
is/In Sumerian
pictographs a diamond
with horizontal line through
its centre thus: ⟐ "means" *legal*
or *decision* or *trial*
or *peace* it is
thought

before a beginning of writing.

A
means of
asking (of heaven)
incised on scapular
bones of sheep
shells
of
turtles
what am I doing?
elaborate calendars
this press to make history
tamper with memory
some one
system
clack-at-a-lack
must have been the earliest

Zulu Dynamite 181

             the first a large rep-
                    ertory
              touch clay pouch
             inside which incised
          on which clack-at-a-ack-at-a
             drawing the threads to-
                gether no sexual
                   feeling for
                     weeks
           read all of *WAR & PEACE* unquote

      calculations / calculus : a pebble   grit   stop.

                  From here:
              pans of creamwhite
             set in green, & green in
              black. Stop. From
                    there:

                   complex
                  florescence.
              Stop. Ripple spreads
            small circles on flat sheen.
                Why did such a
                   repertory

                      of
              three-dimensional
            symbols come into exist-
              ence anyway? In
                  the first
                   place?

                 And how?
               Sipping at the
            honeypot of his mind.

          Is there life after a hangover?
                  Stand back.

Allocations & transactions
clack-at-a
click

drawing
threads together
development of a recording
system developing two
by two

spheres half-spheres disks cones cylinders
tetrahedrons ovoids clack
triangles rectangles
bent coils
bi-

conoids
& schematic
animals scored &
non-scored
quote

He who fornicates with a She-ass inside the Agadir in view of the porter, or in view of any other witness (in whose testimony reliance may be placed) will pay a fine of 2 *dirhem* to the Oumanas & 3 *sa'as* of corn to the She-ass.

Unquote
clack-at-a-clack

represents a logical step
in the
evolution of a system
of
record-keeping.
Stop.

And with the rise of cities
& development of large-scale trade
this system was pushed

onto a
new track so that
images of the tokens
supplanted the
tokens

themselves.

o

Boulders – desert – music – even this
slit – surgically –
   opened & again opened
ground down, carved it would seem,
destroyed it would seem, again,
to a secret beat on the edge of delicacy, reconvenes –
it reconvenes & grows again/one-two/ – again when
who passed where, a fennec fox,
the creosote bush, again.
As on an old tin
roof – tiny whisper of a little rain.

. . .

Another experiment – *spumante*.

o o o o o

And in the pumice that does float, bubbles are
separated from one another by thin films of glass
so that air is trapped inside. Sometimes, when
a volcano erupts in the sea, massive carpets of
floating pumice accumulate on the waves & can drift
a long way off. These may be the "floating islands"
of seafarers' tales, the "astonishing insight" of

blurb review echo-chamber's hazy garbles, carried
thousands of kilometres & washed up on some distant
coral strand.

o o o o o

Is patience alone any good?

o o o o o

Walled in by aggressive chit-chat (the surface of
the chair brown, its undersurface prismatic),
sound of the solar wind, brief squeak of a
daffodil appearing, ptolemaic poetry … I stopped
short, seeing this colourful character cocking an
ear wanted murder, as well as another beer.

o o o

the yellow logbook

A sodium lamp glows in a laneway outside, rose … orange … dandelion. Pause. Detach. The house is quiet. My children sleep, my wife sleeping. We plan to leave this place soon, the outrageous rent, the stinking toilet, the born-again Xtian landlord. No sound. 1 a.m.…

LOG

                                                                  listening

If you throw away your weapons
some less scrupulous person
will pick them up – but

what is the name of the sound of the rain?

(none   a bell)
or anything echoing
between
one thing & another

one thing
of course

one thing

cedes to another
& stored
in

as a matter of

certain

coarsely sometimes
strangely
of

(tap)

course

one thing leads to another

fine
through certainty
in a sort of constricting ring.

I thought the other hammering
was the echo of another(tell/told)
until the first(which?)stopped

(watch)from under which continues(which?)
the other. thing. in time.
as if sound were
visible
to us.

zero is the opposite of one
yes?

& one thing bleeds
one thing leads
in

into another...

water falling from the sky
is one of the most
important of all
of all phenomena that make life
life possible on land
possible

        [Machine   Art   Battle
chores   cores
  (but who can pay yr rent on yr *puppenhause?*)
                                                Cheers.
cures:
     Leisure   Licence   Pleasure

                                        but –
    then a man walked down a street
    then he walked into a shop
    then he took out a revolver
    then he demanded the contents of the till
    then he left
    then he slipped quietly out of the area.
    then he was never seen again.
    This ensures That.

a man is wearing a white cap
with a black peak & white
socks & black shoes. he's
hoping to get money to get
alcohol to get drunk by getting
cars to park in place precisely
where their dance in special/not
any other miracle

                                        but –
those many falcate shadows cast
mesh & web
are indeed the flickering totals of yr
imaginary bank deposits in Dublin
Mombasa.

    fat world
    curled up along one voluted mirror-surface
    administering to/admiring itself deaf
    blind, stupid. click.
    destitute world
    a totally different total amount
    of moment knowing
    moment, yes.]

[sometimes the facts almost *are* the emotions.

I'm leaning on a balcony rail overlooking a
large house across the street. this evening's
a holiday in this country & the new occupants
of the refurbished house are entertaining guests
for the first time under the somewhat soulless
glitter of its new chandeliers. every morning
for the past two months now their workmen woke
us a little too early for neighbourly good cheer,
while the owners slept elsewhere.

their daughter is animated. she is wearing an
elaborate dress. expense as a category, neither
beautiful nor ugly, an exclusionary placard, blatant:
this costs this much & sets me here, you there, or
with me – to bristle & enfold.

my wife & I worry about our debts & our spirited
baby daughter. & the difficulty of getting out of
this mess & learning the language & dodging main
streets at rush-hour so as not to run into anybody
we might owe money to.

their guests are animated, courses served on silver
platters, father at the head of the table, he
seems not very much older than myself (but don't
let's confuse fascination for envy), there is talk
& movement &/but, from here it is utterly silent –
listen – & sad. ghosts…

sometimes, the facts & the emotions blur.]

opening a window there is this

audible creeping edge of rain that
moves over houses vegetation slate
steel earth each with a note to strike
back here always pleats into it thinking
different/difficult (too) being all but up to
you but water especially in this way in this country

river   the simplest thing in
the world the sky
                 sometimes
but worth it when it
gives underwater feeling
push

so that one thing leads to another
& another leads to a thing just so.

yr weapons are
by the way
patience privacy
doggedness.

in the name of the sound of the rain.

great cycles

cued in to the beat of the universe
for direction –

the great cycle we call the year
in temperate zones –

direction
    I was lost
    I was depressed
    I was down & out
    suicidal

iv yoo haf a güd vife he said, smiling.
the worker from Stuttgart.

so:
imperilled love
that pearl
& talking to you can be hard
on love
letting the only things relevant
(difficult) through   so that
so far as words go
then after
then afterwards
to be able to live in
& feed on
up to
this envelope you are
in *happy happy happy*

celestial ragtime
        continental drift

but limited
in that/a pollengrain
settles tectonic the
dustpool moves don't
breathe did you
hear that?

LOG

                                                                                     place problems

Yr screen fills with white print on bright green & other fake precisions outside yr window from yr back to foreground facing the green & luminous machine facing the window, that ruined building across the street, the sky, tantamount to/in which a bird, print, flits.
Take it easy.

Driving into that picture of a lemon not the -ness of this travelled fruit on the table on the billboard with 2 bright nipples or ears to each side this is not it. It's cold & difficult in your cave. It's very cold & difficult in your cave.
Here, then.
.

                    Branches overhead &
                    around reflected in
                    wet tarred camber
                    underfoot. Small Walker
                    In Vein. (Study)

.

imprint of seawave in the white, thin, parallel
gills of the. grains of grit, white, white-yellow,
in turn turning the
grains of.
the webbing held in the frozen undulance of the.
off the into the coast of Zanzibar a while forever. (coral) the.
.

Water droplets that spread & cling then
slip down a windowpane unzipping
a slit on glass to a grey day outside.
Many of these things, many of these things
are roughly vertical, roughly parallel, to the gravitational
centre, the gravitas. And completely artificial.

198 *Zulu Dynamite*

Hand-clapping to their dance
in the dust in the sun
magnifying sweat on their pointed breasts
gleaming smiling moving their torsos
kneeling all in one up-swell
clapping & drumming
stamping & clapping
in the white dust in the red dust
yellow dust grey dust

so that suddenly I can see
you & I can see
the flowers inventing the bees
an instant.

    Elsewhere:
    snow in a bird's nest
    at dawn by the door.
    At night, suns.

the red notebook

LOG

zulu dynamite

In a corner of yr room – to work hard,
any chance you get, privacy, patience –
in a corner of the room His Imperial
Majesty is rummaging through
His folders. Aye. This in the fairytale
of the Valley of Tears. Now & then advancing
ambulances bounce back their sirens
in that dance of violence improvised & manic
etc etc & now & then His little ones shift
in sleep in their palace-to-let on the
racing earth; otherwise, apart from some
paper-sound, silence. Inchmeal. This:
the use of the eyes in spiritual exercises
(A Study):

a charcoal sketch/////unemployed, passable education,
late thirties, father, husband, poet *erase erase erase*
participating at that long remove. As local as that.
I mean: everything run through this tensely amalgamated
shadow-corps so that so many young practitioners
don't even know how much's been filtered out or that
anything has been *erase/erase* in the first place.
Contact. Toy-like parallel movements. So complete, so
concerted has been the walling round. To call repetitive
clones "innovators" & get away with it. To inculcate
a pathologically low tolerance threshold for complexity,
& be thought intelligent. To/but. Don't let's get too.
I mean, sifting the word *if* for many years brings clarity,
maybe. Flecks & spherules…

one: no snakes so
slaked thirst
on burst melon
in shadow
of hollow baobab trunk
fat & marvelous
ly ancient,
a sacred place to go
to the Kikuyu say.

…takes you to here.
snip each corner
of the envelope
with a sharp scissors
making four brown-papered
triangular packet hats
like em … Robin Hood's
but not green.
three, four apertures.
a pert kiss
involving the tongue.

frag
ment
ed
  ly
dent
    ed
rag
time   piano

is definitely not it.

(coda)

dust devil's
spindle spiral
question marking the plain

then disappearing again.
the Basotho kids
don't like it though.

& two: somebody arrives.

         suitcases on the floor.

         the floor is used to it

         & yr table. & the wine jar.

         moving in over the stones
         of the floor
         in a breeze
         dust in under the door
         quietly
         quietly moves past

            (yr move)

         .

         the windy city
         is mighty pretty

         the wind in the city
         is mighty pretty

         .

         & then footsteps
         & a gate
         & then another door closing
         & then footsteps
         & the gate
         & footsteps

            (to hell with the city!)

         my friend, the fridge,
         my friends, the sounds in the street.

dust in under yr feet
as you move in the half-garden
in the red dust alive in a cone of wind
over the plain.

if you throw away yr weapons

some less scrupulous person
will pick them up again.

.

(noise)
    song
(noise)
    song
of the fridge
in waves
noise
of my lips
parting
        noise of …
        clouds moving

  (check)

my friends
(are)
my friends:
        incisors
        mandibles
        teaspoons.

& one: a pigeon lands on a chimneypot
perks its tail up then
down
finding the centre of gravity.
good thing too.
shits.

chipping
at the paper-face
fact
    if   if   if

if your sights are quite low enough,
you'll get by. quite. spicules enter
the skin, snap off so the poison/is
this what you study? our hunt is on.
complexity being tidal, total, when
you catch it looming through fog…

if you think you've got The Answer, if
the answers are patent, if you find
yourself impelled to adjust the world
(just a bit), if you begin to
hope, I mean *really* hope you can slip
into this festival quietly with grace
& a few things still left in the brain
then/I enter, he's on the phone, glances
Ciao! Un attimo, eh? Siediti. /Ciao Marco.
      Va bene. Grazie.

if a boulder lay in the path of one of
the furrows, Zulu women built a bonfire
under it, heated it until it glowed, then
doused it with pails of water. voilà. the rock
shattered. Zulu dynamite, they called it.

dream: I am
that condition in the city
under covering eucalyptus
in the sun
waiting for a taxi
to anywhere at all
unconspicuous

oh help me
help me through the gridding
on the map
stars are skidding
and the sun is dead
and through my head
flames

that
hopeless stab at
pragmatic eutaxy
you taught me
to believe possible
on earth –
bullshit.

wait:
I'm willing to begin
to draw a line
around what's possible
again & go on
with that
from there –

airborne
stones hit glass
crack sky, splinter
slick reflections
of ages as they pass
or get worn
out or die

or/I'm listening
for that creditable theory
on the locked shadows
of empathy & regress
fear & pity
sweat glistening
under the hairline

straining, eager,
academic notetaker,
sensitive earpiece,
intrepid sticker,
lump of ice –
but, still unimpressed,
get me out of here.

Switch on the lamp. Whine of mosquitoes
cruising up & down outside the net. Laugh.

> One two
> one two four
> three.

the dun copy

Table facing a square window
inset in a deep white wall
of a quiet room
on loan to me
(close your eyes)
for a time here
now
around which the
whisper sometimes
of my travelling pet fly
the sun.
Thin line of light
from roof on gable
connects
and silence
and space
what everything insinuates
I have neglected nothing
unquote
not everything in its place

                              waves?

Grooves.
    Dusk
    in the middle of a city
    small city
    darkness due late in June
    a thin line in rhythm
    what next?
    and swallows at great speed
    from Africa
               to Rathmines

Between air
and where air and smoke are
is a coil for the shape of the smoke
to rise in (through) over the leaves burning down
how can we say?

.

It is twenty to twelve by that clocktower.
Twenty to twelve! under a violet dome
in Klee's picture *The (Yellow) Clocktower*.
Between
the pointers on the clockface
black and green
the angle
appropriate to this degree of paradise
a place of
components that glow
in their extension of
a narrow area
a bursting pod.
What is the equivalent of this magic?

A thrush in a hedge in a garden

Sifted scribbles on the backs of travelled envelopes

A hill

A line of trees through distance

Vividly some washing hung out along a rail
bright and beating in the breeze

Wide far empty fields

A few sheep by some fence on a crest   waves?

Grooves:
punctures the skin with a slight sigh
sac of white mucus
curls of worms pink bluepink
a beetle leaving an earthcrevice
skinfilm where tubers were   these things

                          yes

yes
connect
watching the mind in the hand
move hearing the world speak figures.

    .

Pinnate and palmate light and lighter green
and dark green the breeze takes them
direct, briefly, sharply,
swinging
            pod-bearing laburnum
lilac, the "pipe tree".

priority

prior

Sell everything then hope for the best: these
are the basic instructions. The way a root wraps
a rock to a moist crevice sending the bole
up, up to light and leaf, to sky and sunlight.
Each lesson shimmers on and qualifies the next.
So there.

I look at a thread. I watch, I hope, doing the sweatshop
rag (pick up the whisper-movement in the grass, those
insane harmonies of money) and in my hand
mistake everything for everything else: floodlit factories,
fences, dogs, men, uniforms. Maybe I. But. A lax moment
in the zoo. Ready or not, begin.

When your pieces fit moving in the weave they make a
noise together, snug in Disaster Depicted, not Disaster.
Apply the poison. Proboscis, ovipositor, plain

stab-of-the-beak. Under a Tulip Tree, a Jacaranda. Note.

Little human things I remember or can't forget: I
seem to be holding a white pen in my right hand,
thinking How can I trap light with this thing? He
said it was called an "idiot stick", in the army,
referring to something else. Quite right too.

Through and through: a knot, note, is a difficult
concept; witness any child attempting, folding and
winding.

The page nine. Moving in the weave. The Number 52,
moving in the weave. Under the Tulip Tree, the
Jacaranda; little human things, like trying to
remember, a noise, a melody in the mind. Suddenly
I can remember everything (it seemed) (a brilliant
blur): another mistake. Three noises. Five vivid things.

Yr name for the noise of what they were saying doesn't
contain this or the web of the meaning of what they
were saying and this together, shimmering, terrific,
in the grass somewhere. Stay in your building until
this dustdrift clears. Then begin.

Hopeful human mistakes. I think I see what I think
(sometimes), but mostly I imagine where I am
in the dark, feeling around, moment to moment,
ready to respond to elastic surface, do you see what
I hope I mean? A tap on a pipe, an insect clicks;
deep in its pulp, a seed starts out. It's a long,
fantastic journey and nobody *really* believes the
details.

A small tea-stain on your spoon, for instance,
outline, or very near it, of the country I'm
phoning you from and to which you've never been.
What? The ant moves the grain and you have the (that)
headache I gave you again.

Once upon a time there was a story. And listeners
and lines and stories to follow. Once, *olim*. *Fadó*.
Now begin.

A mess of reminiscence is nothing. I was living
on a small half-empty island, cold and wet, and
many poets making much of their mothers and fathers
and grandfathers and grandmothers and fields
and ploughs and pigs as deeply gouged lies – the
surface of Jupiter's Ganymede as I remember it –
in the same breath, phrase-packets, a very I must
say very slowed poetry: this was not Africa.
Procumbent. I left. A weave is something.

I was looking at a picture of traces of colliding
high energy particles from a bubble chamber. Put
your hand in mine (I almost wrote) feel the weave.

A Candelabra Tree has no leaves. Never. A most unusual-
looking tree the book says. It is: my eyes, look. A Tulip
Tree is alright, but the Baobab – now there's a thing!

To get known, affectionately, in esteem, by one's initials,
not carved; printed, repeated, distributed, displayed,
discussed, indeed *flourished* at the end of a work!

To have no readers is hard. None at all. The advantages of
isolation and silence creak in the scales in that old store
where nothing's for sale anyway: *Keep Out* (pale profile
in skeletal light through slats).

Three-year-old Louis, my son, is playing in a sandpit
making me "dinn-ah". I'm extending our Menu each time
he returns, breathless, with offerings, to get some time,
writing on the edge, as I often have to do. He's extend-
ing his world-field, watching, absorbing, making "mistakes"
as we all do. (Are we happy about that?) *Tús maith*.

Enormous woodpiles on these women's heads.
That silent erect cactus, that no-whisper
in the trees' leaves. I had a history.

The lemon tree, the grapefruit, the lime:
watching complications, trying to find,
to tug at a masterstrand in the web. Now –
hey – that's ambitious. Acknowledge this arrowhead
in a dustcloud as your van to Odzi, the future,
invisible – but the map? What's that in a swamp
of metaphor! Moving in the weave. And beat
each other senseless with Love.

They got to know each other, doe eyes to doe eyes,
touched in shadow and sunlight and sweet stimulus
and – what exactly crushes their permanent, delicate
bridges to splinters? (pulp?) They beat each other
senseless with lovemaking in the weave, is a repeating
pattern given time. A mild curative breeze begins. Begin.

Into that shadowy shop again this morning –
take a seat – flat hard inhospitable things,
I know, but bear with me, we don't have many
customers and we don't encourage them, as you know
(half warning, half compliment): *Welcome.*
On our scales here then we have the Names of
the Ingredients against their Idea, which I'd like
to weigh this morning against the alienness
of these to the human mind – are you with me?

Not mad and mannered, taking care what you write,
maybe you've been in too many places and need peace,
stasis, already, but is there *any* utterance that
curves, pliant (I've long ago lost my taste for
bottled poetry) not filled with air-bubbles?

Behind the baroque swimming shimmer of slices of what
there is I think I know what those flat maps spell.
Reality, war-soaked, boiling in a heat-haze?
(& this gives you that headache again?) Tentatively
watch, controlling your nightmares, your self-erected
traps, thorned, horned, ridiculous and deft.

Begin: an inventory of engaging rubbish is this gleaming
ambiguous hoard under the floorboards of that book
in yr dream in the dark: smell of old wood split open –
a muffled, sad crack – and dry-rot. Rhythmic
stridulations of all these different little beings build up
in the air an orchestral alien-ness: human-man-man
it says I hear I say it says, realizing, in a place called,
for the map makers, Odzi. In my shadowshop the scales,
my bright & brittle scales, creak: what is the mindprice
of what.

How can I not care for what you believe, care –
grainbins, cave paintings – but please not pictures
of pictures of pictures, acquired against caring.
Less than a fruitbat's fart in the dark, measured
(with wry, exaggerated care) on the delicate scales in psi.

We came upon it through a hilly thicket, snake-place,
spiritplace, huge overhangs, boulders placed on edge
by a God at play in the dreamtime, swollen roots of
trees out of pure rock – a wonder against nature – here,
hidden, 2 grainbins, paintings, a single claw of a
black hawk. Quietly our children. Begin descending.

This is my desk. This is where I work.
I'm scraping candle-grease off it and
brushing away dust that blows in
through cracks during dry spells in the rainy season.
I work hard in my corner, any chance I get,
really I do.

There's an insufferable smell of shit in this small
box which is called, with no sense of irony, my "study".
Wind bringing in again what we leave out again.

And I've been busy. Busy eating, drinking, giving ear,
listening to repetitive nonsense, setting out, getting
a living, watching my children, teaching my children,
making Lesson Plans, filling paper. But do I ever
learn anything? And if I ever do, do I remember it?
Breath, breathe, breath, breathe…

interlude

THE SIRENS
a ballad

Everything *correct*. And no
use. Facing a tree
in bloom.

Playing the trombone.
Broken glass blood-
stains

spiked fences desklamps dream-
homes/I/Is it. Between
the laws (chance)

(the twisted chain)
(chance)
or:

how many kinds of colour
have you? Or have you
any?

Lithified beach
densed starscrap
touched

with yr feathery mobile hand
chipped metallic
blank.

I mean as far as I can see
that's as far as I
can see.

A spider eating jagged
shadows under a
leaf

raindrop crystal
at the drip-
tip.

In a shimmer of
hollow surfaces
at so many

removes from
so-called
reality

in the unworld
where *Unity*
is

and True/False
tremble
in

the ring – darkness/
coyote
scat.

Let a skeleton set off
then down
a

laneway through a gate and
be gone. Gorgeous Art!
Joints

click. Blank. Dancing
an after-image
on the

retina out of silence
and back into it
and out again

and away curved zagged original
good/good-
bye. *And.*

Of the many links in the set
of all things
plural

that make up
the twisted
chain

i ngile an tráthnóna
i mainistir na
feola

sirens thread the streets
ferry the
dead –

dying – injured – past where
you live (repeat)
(clack)

to the table in
the corridor
or

slab
in the
dark –

splash of
vomit on
the path –

pleading for the sound
of thinking when
the sound

is the sound of no-one-there
that sound –
a

crack in a rock
where ferns
grow –

echo of sap-conducting
paradise in the
shadows

a dog in the dark
cat vanishing from a
sunlit ingle

to brush your ankle
as you pass: *mine:*
keep out.

See! said the Mirror
we are civilized –
subtle urbane

tolerant witty –
holding a pen
just – cheerful

and vigorous
(comma comma comma)
like that:

here we are. Whereupon there
rose up a thing
called

Order – the giant
spinning in his
skin –

AW. DAH. Our adventure had got
under way then out of
hand that's true.

Blue damselfly. Rock at my back.
Secret police. That.
And then

this.
Half-remembered
light-flashes

sky –
grass – trees –
bad

and then good.
What you get
is the Clear

Possible made disappear
by one shifty
manipulator

after another but
the point is/
one two

one three four
two/disclosing
an opening chrysalis

(air bubbled
 in the bones of
 birds in flight)

just to breathe
    and live

sing/passing a little
fruitshop on a corner
by the lights/

    the sirens.
    Yr move.

    ooo

SEAR SEARCH

I'll go down
I'll go down now
down to people walking
talking face to face eye to eye
I'll go down now tonight among them.

Hey – *raghaidh mé síos ag lorg daoirse* –
looking for locks chains impositions
writing listening taking note
25 years 25 years now

bottled up. *Is raghaidh mé síos anocht.*
Tonight. Look down there. Caught.
Pack of dogs – in the loneliness –
of –

of wherever you are & on the dot.
Fixed facade/cut stone & the hands on the big
(joke of a) clock – *ha!* – exact.
Tonight. I'll go down tonight.

Is that thing depression? It's a depression.
Or anger or both. *Ó fanfad libh de ló is d'oíche.*
Is beidh mé íseal, is beidh mé dílis

d'bhur snabsmaointe. Usual ABC. Know what I mean?
In the quiet in the mind
in silence

listen
listen to what is thinking
as it locks unlocks locks.

That's it. Things inside things inside things
inside is the world in discipline
& delight.

I'll go down: tonight. Yes.
Tiny animate creatures connect. Proliferate.
This house; that star. Bless

the smoke
dispersing in the air.
Be desperate. Measure measure.
O fix sticks in mud: decide. Stuck.
Raghaidh mé síos anocht.

SONG

Good.

Huge eyes of the dragonfly
spotting food so far away

fingers keyboards territory ego

all that sweet stuff in buried pulp
chipped from the world compacted

fingers keyboards territory ego

eggs in the broodpouch & in the dune-
grass tiny seasnails eating

fingers keyboards

smooth illusions in their big machines
sugars + phosphates in the chain ring round

territory ego

make a rainbow startled to begin
fingers to the keyboard listen to nothing happening

listen to it well listen
to creaks & clicks

in oldfashioned Advice territory
ego tiny seasnails eating

my river the giver staying put

fingers and keyboards.

Good.

Interlude

*over &
through*

*everything you hold on to in life
is only so many bags of rubbish*

OVER

…after death suddenly the dead. Suddenly it is
irrevocable, that's one of the mirrors. Another
surface reflects that trail you leave in your own
life, a whirl of diagonal stabs in sand. Don't
disconnect! Be with creature-movements. Into
the tree, into the branch & leaf, morning mist,
droplets, spider at the centre of its web,
a slight tickle on your face as a web breaks
onto your skin and you enter the world with a
whisper *ah!* After death suddenly the living.
The surface-tension breaks.

Quietly, quietly to behave about the spirit-dance.
Little chance otherwise others will listen to you.
Two or three small things, small, smaller, enmeshed.
Shed! Shed it all! sings that strange bird I know of
in the banyan tree. Quietly, quietly…

Does matter stop at its edges? In a forest of false
options your picture of the world inside your head
is manipulated from outside to sell you a kind of hell:
step onto that Desire-Wheel and start making and saving,
making and saving, losing and making and losing again
over the checkerboard. What stimulates what? I saw a
snail on glass with a succulent leaf at the other side of that
barrier and thought … of our old friend, Distress, even
at any, even at this stage, coming back to salt the trail.

IN THE MUSIC

The flower of the banana tree is amazing.
Let me say it again: the amazing flower of
the banana tree. Discovering the amazing
flowering banana. Keeping it in mind. Yellow
and purple light in mind. Ox heart on
drooping penis-like stalk, finger-like
bananas in the heart, growing. On the banana
tree. Those shade-giving leaves. In Lesotho
the term *banana* in Sesotho means *girls* and
has nothing at all to do with our yellow,
nutrient fruit. *Banna ba bona banana,*
"the boys see the girls", is its music.
In the fruit in the language in flower.

RESPONSIBILITY

Even that malicious fairytale of division for which it
stands – without a mind – on the cupola or by
the carpark to the pub is nothing to it. The flag
is lucky. It didn't invent itself. It is almost
beautiful, and that is nothing. It is a rag in weather
and that is nothing. It proclaims beer or a people
or both and that is nothing. *Slap slap* goes a cord
on a pole wearing down sounding like a yacht in a harbour
as best it might so that there's only the wind and it
or only the sky and it. Listen to the crack of its fabric
above traffic spitting fractions – stars, colours,
suns, moons – a seamless litany of so-be-it's. And
that's definitely not it. And it may know that. Or
we imagine it might. Or would like to. To transfer some
of the anger. To ameliorate the desolation.

MATURITY

Daybreak: patter of feet to bathroom and back.
Quiet. Contemplation can come from the toes up
to meet child-energy in the head. Rosettes of
data embed the crystal, shattered similes,
useless blurs but ... spalling, advection, cloud-
trails, tidemarks, a swallow in autumn. Mid-day:
bees, wasps, hoverflies tamper at nectaries I
myself bend to examine looking for stimulation
in the garden. We go out for a walk my kids and I.
(Fat bananas clustered where the flower was, troughs
and pockets in the head.) Life, bright and brief!
Tiny meandering pollen shadows, pocked, minūte
circles, diced geometric figures, deeply gouged
brilliant identity-echoes, under the flightpath, up,
wheels dip, flaps down, a steady waver in the great
machine where jets make landfall and go on. My children.
One by one by one. The trees' canopies curl over us,
bend and sway at the sky's lips. Of course. Our
children fly. Fragrance rises. Stem wavers.
World turns. One. Back from the retina shoals of
information slot into place and, from its stone out,
one pollen-grain, one, the fruit's flesh swells.
Delicious! Yellow, the daystar; green is begin.

SOUND

I wish I had a house, wheedle and whine, I wish
I had a bit of money, closing the door,
opening the window. Soul's ability
to ripple through crisp watermarks – vertical
layers – mud and wattle cabins and a tidy
compound. Only a house. In. The.
Breathing. For instance. I wish I had a
roof, my two kids, my one wife. Less
nomadics, but then a whole haversack
of heartstopping examples: wash-basins,
wainscot, rain-pearls on a clothesline,
a clean spread of glasspane deep in its framebed,
whatever you've got, a folded view through
gold and developing veins underground,
small traditional poems – or even less
traditional poems even – or even less.

RAIN

A folder falls open. Isolate and know the details.
Flower-like cup at shoot apex. Who is running
their wars? With whom am I safe? The child, despite
everything, takes everything in. Be warned.
Then a folder falls open: drained gear oil sump,
refilled it, bled the brakelines, all set to take wing
on up through Matabeleland. In this heat the Limpopo
all but dry.

A folder falls open: ebony butterfly, blue shocks,
glazed vermillion centipede flowing – elongate –
up a tree. My face pale in a window, at the controls,
eerie glow. Rain and wind. Zooming through hurricane.

And falls to the floor ... flysong, birdsong, cloud-
movement. Sunlight in a stream. The way the water-surface
plaits and pleats. A dragonfly nimble in undersurface
silence though its wings almost never co-ordinate.
My daughter. White gables among trees, leaves bright
and green and dark-veined in the light.

Legislation is the rules of the fight, a rondo in
plot-pages, not a comfort, honey, or didn't you know?
Opulently produced by. Irk and then manipulate. Beware.
Oh?

Deft needle-beak of the weaver-bird flitting bits of
grass through and through into its cosy upside-down
calabash swinging, making for its mate a chambered
showcase. Contact. Otters on their backs in a river
cracking out food. Stones. Gulls crabs another way around.
A monkey's grassblade trickily siphoning living nibblets
from an anthill. Succulent. Flints, axes, arrowheads...

Then earth quarrelled with sky and sky became
angry and withheld rain. And life on earth began to
dry up and die. Then earth sent a bird to sky

and the bird pleaded with the sky and sky relented
in the end and sent rain. Tentative rain, contending
rain, unbending rain, amending rain, attentive rain,
a tent. Of rain. Question-mark, dart and date. Point,
hack. Circles and arrows. Flint instruments. Needled,
need I say, a stolen music. Not poetry. The point is:
hand over those beautiful garbles. City washed and
scintillant after it, a gully opening up.

SONNET

This is the house I live in now. Dance. Through
data in the Dust Veil Index. Twenty years clothes
waiting in a wardrobe, wind in the trees cont-
acting in tit-for-tat communiqués, sweat sticky
on the eyelids. What's going on in or who's
winning this game of Pinnacles and Hollows now?

A country uncle sees an imitation African mask
on a windowledge and thinks: Devil Worship!
Precisely. My tunnel is bigger than your tunnel.
In extent, furniture and decoration. Come in.
What's new?

This is the house I live in now. It is to be poor.
It is to be decided on without grounds. It is to
spend one's life thinking, and be thought an idiot;
to live by dint of intensive works, and be thought
lazy; to cherish one's wife and children and
be thought ga-ga. Dance! The grub feeds on the egg,
fat enough then to step down onto the appropriated
honeypool in the cell. See through a delighted
entomologist's eye, delight, discovery. Cracks the
mud-wall, flies free.

In pieces, of a piece, piece by piece, pieced toget-
her, pax. *Do-chum glóire Dé agus onóra na hÉireann.*
And digging at the back of the house – *hah!* – cloud-
bands on the Jovian planets, rusty of-which's, a gnarled
else-tag by a breeze-block wall. Look, wait, I…

RAIN

Any number of incidents blurring these tiny peaks.
Believing our own eyes watching the image, the
fine film, the regular wedges. Watching what I
see I feel uneasy suddenly because of the. It's
the fragility. It's because Of The Fragility. No-
body else. Tiny dry gulch overhung with palm and
cactus down there. Prickly Pear/Indian Fig in flower
further along. Further along this eloquence gets
dangerous ... History-whispers, emotive mutterings,
do ghlam nach binn. Ash-tree, crab apple, damson,
hawthorn, bramble, the delight spreading, inchmeal.
Click.

That was his life. After so many years away from it
to read again the names in that language, his language,
as any, anybody's, a "dying" language, a braille
following the mind to the spot where your fingertips,
older, colder, bolder, more hungry, descend. To
*nóinín, neantóg, bainne bó bleacht, feochadán, sabhaircín,
fraoch* ... It moves and flits. Bits stay in place.
Bits recombine. Bits underpin then vanish in the argument,
fite fuaite ... *An tosach, ar deireadh.*

Is one negative presented in the dark. The rains
break on the tin roof, peeling a piece of bark to
get the smell of the tree feeding, the imminence of
storms, the next page turning, a flicker of lightning –
graphite, cork, dust – just as the substance-strata
stagger to the music when everything's evanescent
in its timeblock before going on to pretend that.
That the meaning of meaning (split) matters.

SONNET

You rise of a morning, early, shirt,
underpants, pants, sandals, in the half-light,
quiet. Toilet. Downstairs through hall,
kitchen on tip-toe, through the garden
to the shed at the back of the house
with your bundle of papers. Beginning
is a change of sound and that changes things,
and things tell each other where you are and
how to be and – how do you feel about that?
Blackbird on a wall.

There was a voice, casual, some man
humming some tune, but nobody at all
anywhere about. Later, a little while,
entering a busy street I'm beside a man I
recognize, from years back, humming exactly
that tune, in the fabric, to lock in(out)(as
it were) that extra sense; greedy for that extra,
scavenging at the fence.

o

Luminous beetle, crimson spider, widowbird's long
black kite-tail curving down to cover in the grass.
That birdcall with its weird whistle at the end…
Instep, step. Echo. Undercloud, overcloud pass noise-
lessly in your time of study, head down, from
the heart, the first instructions, *And.* And
going about your business: handedness, symmetry.
That blue in the sky, that white, that off-blue.
But what's this in that shopwindow there, ghost-people
connecting with ghost-things shimmering and going by?

RESPONSIBILITY

Step into the wet garden under the leaves
of the sycamore drenched in honeydew.
Enter that garden by a black gate
in a green hedge. A book is a
paper object out of place in a garden.
Contemplation's ok. Who placed that book
at the back of the wet garden in this ardent
picture of abstraction? What is a holy day
in this context? Whose shadow is that
in this nook? Without contemplation, zero.
Ah yes. A mesh of surface tension. I mean
a web. Of green of blue. Mind your head.
And then something else.

A drench of energy crackling along the
fibres on an island within an island,
bridgeless. My father will die not knowing
I lived as I did because I. But. Even
here. Telling him. Listening for a
no-answer that's always there. Telling
him. What's my pen doing down beside *that*
crevasse anyway? Deaf in this icy air
another deafness burns through to where
the vulnerable skin is bare. But that's not all…

IN THE MUSIC

Suddenly I could hear
distinct each wingtap that
a butterfly made quite
clearly quite a way off
coming this way

then about & past again
around my head while the street
I was in to amuse my son
with a racquet & ball
just as suddenly developed

an echo it never before had
taking what I thought I was
saying stopped by a web under a
windowsill the (three-one,
two-four, tap) the/this –

it's in the language, yr pocket,
the back of yr head – silk-dab,
paddle-dip – taking the
sounds & giving them back ship-
shape quietly into the world

where waters slap & fan:
a pink hand in a red cloth
polishing a brass plate on a brick
wall: *Director of Public Prose/...*
"Do you like it?" –

the/this spider failing with its
prey sailing away, music,
dance, winning out again (postbox,
gable-end, walltop) anyway.
Write to me soon. Do.

POINT

Love plants peace. Not a catalogue of manipulative
fairytales. Sky gives back. Gable-shape, tree-lines.
The way the sunlight is, the way it comes down
through leaves, and spider-silk gleams and
doesn't suddenly, between lightly moving branches
in the morning to be still. The order of the stones
in the wall beside a yellow dust-track magnified,
the insect ready, then away over and through a light
dustfall in a sideways breeze gone but, very small,
is noted. *Gósta garbh-Bhéarla:* brief spillage of
birdsong. The first second. The others are different.
The others are written down. *Ah whoom* goes the
orchestra, *spang!* goes the Giant's buckle, *wisha-wisha*
go the trees in the grove. Hope, it is hope, and a glow
without a name, Mary, envelops all those places we've
ever lived in, been to, but never – *let the cloning
begin!* – presumed to own.

FIRE

I was walking through the rain with the electricity money in my
breast-pocket, head down, past cinema, school, shops, houses,
hotel, church – grey, greyblue, black – mist rising, Tuesday.
Out of the sun in the red dust by the rondavel my daughter
can do all the clicks of the language. Palate and alveolar ridge,
energetic young tongue chops the breath-cells. Baroque fog.
Recitative rain. Hope. Look! there! a Language Poet grins &
flickers in the ghost of svarabhakti in the west of Ireland,
risk misting the screen. Pushy, pugnacious. But there's no
murder in my heart today. As I was saying, I mean, more lyrically
speaking, and years ago, and elsewhere, of course, if still part
of the same tune, and moving, as in a whisper, to the main events, this

> *silver black sometimes lime the trees*
> *& all the time the roof of the annex*
> *is bright silver*
> *the top surface of its oiltank silver*
> *an adjacent roof greysilver greyblack*
> *as silver flies move quickly*
> *through other colours*
> *& back*
> *where everything that can gleam*
> *instantly can darken too.*
>
> *rain pelting resistant windowpane*
> *wind on roof*
> *& the narrow ceiling over where I am we are*
> *taking the trees*
> *talking to the trees speaking peace*
> *brushing the outer structure of the house*
> *kissing the wound of the cut tree*
> *somehow crumbling reforming not ours not despair*

A malachite sunbird by a minaret plant by a window, the flower
of the Victoria Lily that locks a feasting beetle in.

MATURITY

Root-things speak to the music to be made to
commune with, not myth-luned, disunitary, buried.
Up they pop: books, readings, fans, jobs, prizes.
Down they go: unpublished typescripts *plop*
on the floor. And from your shopping-list in the
bottle: fear. (Defeat.) Curled, spread. Nobody
is a fool. What is it we call thinking anyway,
brushed by rhythmic cilia, Heidegger in the shadows,
Rudolf Diesel in the workshop? Balance? Take a
walk! Up starts the engine, I open a book,
sit back, steady a page, sigh. Am I taking in
the wishes of the master choreographer accurately?

Camera shots is not living, however. Unbelievable
that may seem. It must be said. Skimming shallows
where swallows were tracking I/or but if I
knew where that anger came from then maybe I could.
Slice through the root to a new cloud-life below
that. Quite below that, far.

SOUND

Deep into the furrow of a single underwave
won't give you the sea despite what they say.
They say "corner, corner, corner, corner"

>crumple up a tissue & dust yr
>desk make a space even the
>paper you write on is damp dhow
>past window starlings on branch
>all this action agitated western
>whiteman with a timetable for a
>spine fiddling about with his
>car its locks & clocks 9 a.m. all to
>a small piece of/head down, at the
>work, when out of nowhere, a bell

>>listen: hammer taps
>>seam glistens

Item: pencils, pen, desk. Paper. It's good to
see you again this morning citizens ... activists!
Death is nothing. There's the soapstone dish
from Mombasa, the undulant mushroom coral from
Prison Island, Zanzibar. *Item:* in the middle of
November, short, cold days. Pause, detach. Death
is nothing at all. Even among this filthy species.
Item: a window a mesh to test the soul, a door
a blaze of heat and light, burst of energy at a
twigpoint, readiness in the ash-tree's black stops,
pliancy in the toplines down. Down and across...
Close the gate. Close the gate, graciously
close the gate, lovingly, close, ever so, close
it, so, tact, then, do.

A PERSONAL NOTE

Music irritated my husband more than anything else. Forced to hear a stray tune, a fragment of song, or someone whistling, he would throw his work overboard and wreck the inspiration. Afterwards he must begin again from the beginning. That is why at home one never heard music. No one ever sang. No one whistled. That is, unless my husband chose otherwise.

Ainö Sibelius

LIKING THE BIG WHEELBARROW

We sat on a side of a mountain and muttered
something about the Basotho. We were dissatisfied.
We were given a part of something to understand,
our self-esteem under attack, daily nibblings
at the plinth. Fixing bridges, developing struts.
Wait. The instruction was to wait. Be still.

Dust particles collide and bounce away, collide
again elsewhere and stick until a thicker
filamentary delicate medium sinks to the central
plane of a disc which breaks into rings which
clump and accrete which orbit the core which spark
the beginning of the accretion of the solid cores
of the planets we know, from webs and threads
on magnetic bands. In theory. Only quietest
collisions. Clusters. Crystals and dust grains.
A four-year-old child who said to a pilot
on their way to the plane on the air ferry tarmac
"I like your big wheelbarrow."

A PERSONAL NOTE

In a laneway
that once was a road
blackberries hang
red & black

the wren in the ashtree
hiding robin abiding
we pick & take home
fruit in a bag.

Over nettles & wet
grass over the hedge &
where birds pass
over the sky

this planet's envelope
& its dead satellite
over this system & its
ordinary star

elliptics spinning, circling,
to a speck my fingers reach in to
one waterdrop tensed from
heaven on a rosehip.

Take it as a gift. Simplify,
condense, know the inside,
dying, travelling towards you
on its track –

coatings of dry spider-bits on the
windowledge – to focus to where
the seam glistens, the hammer
taps. Listen…

AND THROUGH

Bright berry in a blackbird's beak.

Sun's risen, condensation on the window.
Intermittent birdcalls. Otherwise so quiet
you can hear my/ brush dance (clearly) along
the paper in painting after painting where
I find myself arriving from the other side in,
solar panels glinting (bright berry) against
tympanic black in the vast. Vast…

bright berry in a blackbird's beak

: the Vast. Maybe I did see what that contained, once.
Remember. Rotate. That did include the sea. Spin.
As it happens. Round. On a red dust track tired
and repeating the simple in fatigue of heart and
fatigue of spirit, repeat, the simple pattern.
Involve. Stone outcrops, flat sky. Task: draw close.
Make hope. Don't die:

bright berry in a blackbird's beak.

In time, nothing. Love, work, knowledge. The weapons
are nothing in deep time. In through the eyes, ears –
wing-caressbeats over the landscape – braided rivers –

bright berry in a blackbird's beak.

People have houses. Spaces. People occupy spaces,
radial spokes connect, fold, knot. Conduits, taps,
struts. Their difficult obsession Labelling the Clouds
equals what, however?

Bright berry in a blackbird's beak

o

Each shock each minim of each thing here
cored chord cordate current
a life a labyrinth of glistening
inconsistencies but to *keep* that   kept
each bright at-least each tooth in the zip
each strange thing   its lenticular glow in the distance
a strange thing   bright berry…

  bright berry in a blackbird's beak.

coda

WORK DAY

*...late August early September & between sirens
& through fume even here floats thistledown –
soft, evasive, delicate – as it follows up & past
yr open palm & (come to the edge of a suggestion
of) the beginning of Lesson One.*

You take up the book and you begin again.
Purity. Miracle. It is a clear cool morning
in late November. Washing waves on a line
outside your window and a young tree in an
adjacent backyard holds some withered leaves at the
tips of its thin branches against the blue.
They too move. Lightly. (Already you begin to
cross things out.) Purity. And things get placed
between brackets. In a child-like way. And repeated.
In a child-like way I look forward to having a
livelihood. That too must stop, another fairytale!
Brackets? A church bell in the distance. For all your
hammering: listen. Silent the joy that overwhelms
you when it's finished as different materials
in things around you surround you, link fingers,
radiate: the sensitive blue balloon of the Earth
in Space, that miracle. All day, bursts of fire,
all day.

steps

…agus a haon, dó, trí

i

STEPS

To go in one machine on the road watching
another machine in the sky. To enter the
machine I'm travelling in I entered a card
in a machine going a progress through the
suburbs where all the houses are the same.
Lock hands and hope, let the mood deepen,
step into/down to learn, to change machines.
The one in the sky has entered cloud and
disappears. But the sound…

I see a globe wrapped up in occupied flight-
paths on a screen. I hear the light noise of
the buttons on the keyboard depressed.
The ravine between you and this world you're
supposed to be in wasn't a dream, and. Turn.
Passing an insect on a wall, its supple antennae
already measuring (Time = Energy – Money x Hope).
What have we missed? Who is reporting what
to whom? Turn sharply into the less well-known.

This? A high-pitched melody from a digital watch
on your wrist in the desert. Which type of hype is
the best type, the most manipulative, the most
lie-laden? Gecko, stopped. Beat, pluck, tickle
its rhythm through! A tiny cloud, one bright wisp,
to the west moves – in time, burin nicks – moves
just a little bit, moves me, *ah*.

RETICLE

Move in: a web shivers (my father
swimming in the open sea, those strong,
unmistakeable strokes, link to link) a
dust of scales, greenish purple, towards
the thorax on the bramble stem, edged,
programmed trap, and your fingers tingle.
Take time as a solid. I was alive in and
overhearing what? Step.

Suddenly this morning on the way to the shop
in a blackthorn bush by the railway track
I picked out a birdcall I'd never before heard.
So. Or this afternoon coming back from
the post office the clean whorl of a snail's shell
on a white wall. Stopped. And stopped again,
thanks, to take in five more such on a gable-end,
each different, streaked, polished, echo-ported,
glazing a trail to nowhere in particular just then.

Open your books, checking the bunched items
in the seam, yes, but skirt the piranha pool, that trick
of engagement in the air, thick. Look. Applause and
photographs. Where will a filament fall? What small
breeze take our lives away? I dip my hand in. *Spang!*
goes the Giant's buckle, again.

IN THE MUSIC

When leaves wither and begin to blaze and
fall all the way down the ladder to each
rootweb's radius in a plot they make a brittle
miracle of beginning a paintbox on bright grass,
the die set. There it is, in the slack between
one of the little stopped waves on that tin roof
over where I know its nest is in under the beam
over the window, flea-hunting. Quick-quick, gone.
Log: at your Problem Wall at the heart of the maze,
do not impose your will.

Being all ambiguous cloud-places and so quiet so/
that *is* there could be thought to/I think they/
what's that? trickle on a map, a musaic, (could be
an omen, I mean, amen), cloudberry and hare's-tail
cotton grass, "messages come in flashes", ready or
not. Nonetheless. Perhaps. However. Argument.
Disputation. Dichotomy. All circles, glints that in
their cross-grain/skarns/revert; do not impose your will.

Is it really the 10th? Can't be. Wait a minute. (So
many facts, so much manufacture, so little prey.)
Tipply-pip, says a bird, *do-you-agree, do-you-agree*.
Sometimes, briefly, even here I/or/I do. But then…
A cat in the grass, amity, seedcup.

SONNET

In it build. A wall of tiny, precise, bricks,
a wall of fittings, of feelings, discoveries,
evasive shadows, wall of absence collected,
wall of tears justified, the wall of plain
speaking. If a system locks you to a screen
it directs your life. Leave the room. Breathe
in. The wall moves out a bit. Blue pen, red pen,
many ways through: put that in your pocket
to feel better in times of distress … yes?

An old wine bottle base found in a wall
built a century ago around a house in rural Ireland
now in a case in a museum in a castle in the middle
of Ireland under my odd pink reflection
peering up; with what intention? Click. Sunlight
on a chimney pot. A crow on a roof. Shocked by
shards that fly past my face here: a "career in
'development' ", the "management of the poor".
And lodge in the receptive surface of the wall
opposite and disappear.

MARCHING SONG

Tittle on a drum. A seated figure
at a desk from the back. A ten shun.
A tube of dust. Descending steps. In
sum. It's. It's the way they're always
"they" and never ever ever. Ever.

Plant your feet on the ground as the
basis evaporates in a blur of academic
backchat/I think I/Got that? Turn round.
As if as if as if ... The point of the
story, the point of all his little stories
was, note, *poor me*.

o

As if running could ever stop anyway,
each sour step collecting bitterness at each
failure to pause to close the spaces between
things and their settings, selfish, lazy, blind,
deaf, never growing up, never wanting to,
even their own children sacrificed to
particularly their own children sacrificed to
this ego-dark, this maw. Is the point.
How do you feel about that? Close the book.

Daystar on a branchtip, raindrop holding in.
They'll come, they'll succour and lay siege,
furtive and uninvited in the early hours,
vanishing in a cloud of ionized futures busy
under the sun beginning. Dry sticks, foot-
prints in the dust.

o

(A) Walk away, and their weapons are gone;
laugh at yourself (B) and they bury themselves
in their own muck. Let everything, as it
happens, (C) happen between brackets, and the
brackets (dreaming) bulge, skip, loop.

The sun *block* the moon; the night *block* the day;
winter-spring-summer *block* autumn top; tap trowel,
scrape. The gap between the footsteps on the stoep.

PARTS

slate a blueback stone
"black stone"

chalk a white stone
"chalk"

learning to follow
the way you hear the talk

you will learn to follow
the ways you see talk
deployed

& learn to initiate deployments
in surprise
measuring surprise
crestfallen by the word *is*

& this habit
will facilitate & hinder
yr ideas about the world
skintight   to itself

in the darkness
(&) in the light.

o

to speak in the foreground

fateful relation

to speak in the foreground

not by
   addition
   subtraction

to keep the light ground cored

as conditions amass

as the fate is set

budbursts in the light
as against mass murder

to eke out what the ore can tell

of the dew of heaven
& fatness of the earth

before the end

to speak in the foreground

shiver of calculation

    dark.light

o

the tune of tact
(as you write)
skill of gifting well
(as you speak)
an appropriate pacing

facing the proper way
(in the light).

no dearth of boxes
shiny tight spacious
(ice rosettes where ice is cut
dice caught falling to earth heard knock)
yr life locked in at the edges.

for how long do you plan to
carry *that* contradiction?

o

(2 hands to yr cheeks re-
calling. kiss.

pretty head in a crowd
more alive than
any old petal on a bough.
goodbye.)

o

from stone
lichen
on clear air, coaxed.

IN THE MUSIC

There is a ball, a sphere. There is a field,
a rectangle. At each end a space, an Aperture.
Markings on the field and men, marked and
numbered. A set of rules, a set time, a whistle,
an umpire, an audience. The phantasy of pride of
skill in tactical symmetry, the siphon of violent
energies, bonding of comrades, place-adoration,
display-therapy: our gift, your tradition! A poet
under the grassblades, threnody in the palmtrees.
There is a ball, a sphere.

Giving back a black mesh, all the rules together, connected,
or if all the rules together, dilated, make a path out then/
Then our rules get up and shake hands. Game, set. No

I mean yes. Turn. Tangled up in its geometry a tree
sprouts TREE (in English, but not in Italy). *Chak.* (*Again*
is the sequent matgic.) If, stepping inside around and then
outside and then again inside the circle of the rules of
the game is the game, what then? Got that? *Chak.* But that's
a new game. Turn, dance. Busy, busy, busy

SONNET
the words

They are building a house, note
and accrete, tat-tat. On the map.
That. I. But. Building a place
on a place so that/is yr cell
in yr hive quite adequate? Patches
of leaf. Conduit, shadow. Walling
and windowing, dooring and flooring,
a wandering idiot, humming and
hawing, hello-ing and no-ing, oh
yes. Shimmer of advancing futures,
oily consecutive links, building
a dream on a fact.

Cut down. Lieing in bed, lying in bed.
Games in a laneway – Pluck-&-Recant,
Dip-it-in-Blood – keeping the smooth
hollow of the blowpipe clean,
lap and accrete tat-tat. Building a
house in the air. Then the air moved aside
to the music. And the music come round
wrapped in that. Cut down. Or didn't you hear?
Braided Tunnels, Places-You've-Been-To,
Pivots, Webs, Crystals shiver to the cliff's
edge and over, and then, (just that), and then
learning, dolce, you can fly, dolce, then.
All praise.

But, to recap: a house, a shed, a shield, a tree,
its shadow, appalled, collapsed, afloat, aloof,
amen. Amen, tat-tat. Amen-tat-tat. Afloat, aloof,
amen.

IN PRAISE OF PAINTING DOORS
for Louis' recovery

If your five-year-old son falls from a high wall
to concrete and fractures his skull, concentrate
your love. Focus everything. Everything. Everything,
day and night. Everything.

Afterwards, all going well, leaving the hospital,
take brushes and white spirit. Everything. Don't
underestimate the virtù of the clean rag in your pocket.

White can be a bore, that's true.

On the other hand, a whole lifetime can be a foil (too).

That a conference/congruence of colours in the world
has something to do with the pulsebeat of blood in the
human body might be worth looking into. But not yet.
Hell! *Rag!*

At waist level, sit and paint to your patient boot-top.
Your spine deserves pleasure too, not panic, not despair.

Don't be proud of this house. Obviously … The jackal
solicitor has his fangs in your neck. And there's the
little matter of deep time. Paint on.

Walls speak to doors. Doors answer back. However much
tempted, never intrude.

In the hallway. In the living-room. Oh, and here's one:
"in the 'utility room'". Now where do I live?

My children's feet in their shoes on the floor.

Fly with positive possible energies landing only
to watch in delight.

You too were something once.

Return brushes to spirit. A force in the body of the work demands it. Sit, eat. Ashtree sapling outside in a play-breeze by a window.

Having shed clutter, to the next house go, with a light pocket, a light heart, a light touch, a fire in the mind, and a plan, lightly carried, as lightly let go.

STEPS

He is moving a ladder. He is climbing it.
He is whistling. Sound of a jet.
Sound of someone sawing wood. A cat moves
smoothly along (hammertap of hands fixing tiles
to slats) the granite coping of a cottage
in the laneway. Stops. Disappears over a
rooftop.

Downwind of your nightsky time-probing telescope's
definitely not apples, or clove oil or myrrh!
Chipped granitic plug. Pad along past the lip
of the last grip, let fly…

You'd slept well and rose immediately,
kettle on, bundle of papers out to your shed
at the end of the garden through the dewy grass.
In detail and proliferation (hoverfly's
pulsing abdomen, secret nectary opened out)
a ladybird beetle ambling past through
the proliferate grass. Is that the word for it?
A woodlouse dropped off a door-jamb, so quiet you
could hear it drop.

SOUND

What cruder machine than a machine
you think can listen. The machines get
up and dance, sit down and cry. So it
seems. Withdrawal of information,
distortions, ludicrous non-choices among
snapping fangs. What's this nonsense about
voting? Wake up. Or "Why do men fish
when they're not hungry?" (Leda, 6).

Just before dawn you can think straight.
A good fit, as it happens, apt; bigger vistas,
less credulity. A lifetime in segments
up to that point. Then start again.
A gain. Pliancy. On the other hand…

Sound of a flame flicker, sound of your
scratching your head, listening in. From
the outside of your life, a pattern threaded
through, to the inside of your life, what at
the back of your mind coming to the front,
tautens. Look, I move my fingers. Oh. Feeling
the pull of that nearby star the river twists
and spins. Then I began to walk about with
my body again.

SONNET

1: Move in: shiver. It rises with that strange
crisis of the heat and the blazing moon
in the dark. This is not a conversation with
anything like anything you could like. I
know I know I know the muffled tape downstairs,
practiced blues. Living in tiers. Worry about
worry in a package won't get your eyes
off the microfiche zipping by in a blur.

2: Climbed Kholo Mountain one misty Sunday morning
at a time of year when the initiation schools
were not in session. Herdboys with sticks,
Basotho blankets, outsized rubber boots,
scampered up and down the slopes and sang
initiation songs in caves. We came to a lake
and they gathered kindling for us. Gossip. Gossip,
just under the surface, edging in, through, involving
itself in the flow, sticking its ego-clamp over
the plan, gossiping, gossiping … *Vide cor tuum.*

3: This is a stark shaft of moonlight, one tree
for miles in the dark, on the plain, its shadow, struck.
Durability, scrupulousness and the record; these,
are the three things.

STEPS
the tune

It impinges to such a degree that a minimum
function required to remain the anonymous
human agent in the world exerts a pressure
disproportionate to the results required. *Chiaro?*
Birdsong. I am that perfect citizen. Nothing is
nothing. Yes-ing and no-ing and on-the-other-hand-
ing my way through the mesh. I mean mess. Just
pre-set the dial for Discipline: palm-frond in Harare,
a bridge in Cambridge shiver a synapse.

    o

      adze-cut coral rag
      (2 block sizes)
      lilac spike/key on a string.
      a first floret
      ever looked into
      termite tunnels
                 mimosa flicker

        (coming to
         coming through
         coming round)

      filaments in a ring.

FIRE

Moving through shadows under the trees,
diamonds and islands of light sliding over
a figure disappearing into the dark,
the closely-felted interlocking needle-like
crystals of feldspar with a scattering of
colourful smaller crystals of olivine
and pyroxene and some black specks
of iron oxide/then one. Sharp. Jab. Move,
if you dare. Before you start anything,
stop.

The magic mice make gold. The beautiful
poor girl's hair is gold. A boulder rolls
from the cave's mouth disclosing gold.
Gold, gold. There is gold leaf to each tree
and a rich vein under the forest imminent.
Then I woke up.

Rest your head in your hand. Task: (still)
fill in the spaces between the waves of
that echo. Draw close. Opal. A mango fills
your palm and weights it, scrupulous, before
you bargain, before you speak, before you
breathe again, calm.

IN THE MUSIC

ooo

This route turns sharply under a railway track, then turns again, sharply, up. Look back at the town, the other way. Sit on a limestone drywall. A dog goes by. (*Will* is the tense where the problem is.)/I turn out of my way to take in the laneway to the side of the park to visit sycamore and goose grass, cuckoo spit, placing my foot beside a pool of what sky it catches and touch (travelling) limestone wallblocks, lichen rosettes, that small group to the right of venerable pine, lime and chestnut further on, oh yes, by the court-house. Smile to myself. The fossil record. (Only *will* is the tense where the problem is.)/The light come a long way to play in all these busy, invisible canals goes back – *ah* – memory as an agglutinative wobble of soundwaves? Some time passed

*& then
suddenly we heard again that same deep trumpet-like sound we'd heard from a distance when we entered the lagoon.*

Then a dozen or so men came forward, went into the hut, they were playing strange trumpets and flutes, breathless now, breathless with emotion & delight.

ooo

RESPONSIBILITY

the fid; stirps.

not to write very cold poetry.

that events of social/political significance
be *witnessed* seemed reasonable enough & yet.

ha! pro deo pro patria & the tightening knot
at the top of the spine.

long lines of characteristic compact crowns
suckering vigorously in hedgerows.

they've never had children.

there it is, yr ache, fibrous, gripping the
secret verbum at the basis: *take, take, take,*
kerfed & set into the rabbets.

little nude screams.

coda

in the tree's underchamber
roots enmesh & thicken

(I know   I know   I know)

after white silence
the yellow growthsound

very   quite
delicate listen

FIRE

low sky
gull   aerial
head that way
this
beak wide
calls
    snowthroat
    snowpulse
calls
    then

a crow's
outer wing
upturned
on the
downthrust
in the upwind
a dancer
stepped through
a laneway
one-two

two-five
before you looked
out that little
window
down the
street
in snow
(speck that
 you are,
 babyfist)
pod
oh
glyph-continuing
trackfollowing
one male adult

wind blew
I could tell
this way not

that when/vast
dustmass incub
ating stars/
smell of
catpiss or
what's-it
flowering
currant?
(pod)
& a dog got
about too
quite busy
in its
early morning
check-around.

two shadows
a third
grey ply
black/red
dix-huit
dix-huit
wingflash
wingbeat
well &
good.

low sky.

ooo

a cup of water on a table
table on the floor
the floor on the ceiling
of the next cell down

drizzle continues & then
continues a fine web
revealing fine webs shimmering over
yr table shivering five crumbs of bread

shimmering or prove it otherwise
organized spaces so that
definitely everything we did say
we read we hadn't did they said now.

MATURITY

Smell of cypress in summer, that grey
roof among trees picked out by the sun
on the side of a small hill in distance;
young, in through the eyes, the strong tang
of the world impacting its *itself* on you,
a tide of smallest, simplest things.

The big idea was God. When it first entered
the language meaning *Loud Noise*/but don't let's
get/And a century or two of that kept them
happy. Or quiescent. Or moral. Or stupid. Or
blocked up. One day in the summer of '52; then –
lilac tree in flower – today. Is it raining?

Nothing is nothing. I am your perfect citizen.
Finitude is rubbish, everybody knows that.
No wonder the secret police are busy. Phone me
(to lie in bed Understanding Poetry) phone me
when you get back.

FOUR CORNERS

The language spits pidgin dominance

And from a height.

o

A curious parallel with

Birdsong.

PERMISSION

who, diabetic, prone to gangrene, lost both
legs   bit by bit

whose family abandoned him

whose wife realigned

whose case was taken up

who arrived back suddenly from hospital
in a wheelbarrow

who was constrained to sleep separately

whose gable collapsed in the rainy season but
seemed nonetheless content to live thus
till his son came back from the mines   a tidy
compound & a hard wife

who employed himself with us one day out of the
blue under a tree cutting branches he could
reach for kindling for tobacco money & just never
afterwards quite went away

who got about with chunks of tyres on his stumps

who never missed a party at our place

who must have watched me sit my young daughter
on the slowly disappearing wooden fence of our compound
(quality firewood) of an evening for a chat

whose son came back from the mines in the end &, drunk,
thanked us   florid & a little, somehow, threatening

o

so.

that Threads can intersect at the dead mesh of

Poignancy (yellow dust at my feet, blue
mountains, far sky)(I am quite sensible
to this) if let.

& yet. so.

RESPONSIBILITY

Washing her clothes in a rusty
old wheelbarrow by a dam by a
track under a eucalyptus where
frogs at night fill the village
air with/her bright brown eyes
and mouth connect in a smile whose
radiance and playfulness the fine
skin black/I thought I could get to
know almost everything once not quite
yet feeling the bounce in the net
(The Oxford English Dictionary of
Spraints, Pretoria Encyclopaedia
of Mortgages, Concise Cambridge
Political), when arcane thinking
clicks in its conduit. Tap: "an artist
is *never* poor." Swallow that.

BALLAD

dance of the world in the world is the world
an old steel pump, Victorian, at the foot of a dune
which still gives water   still

o

marram builds   directed   builds
my children too [learn, learn, learn & do]
& that most pliant of materials: questions-&-execrations.

o

under a sycamore, plants on a wall, a fly dipping
its head into nectar, sources swaying, shimmering,
systems, structures melt & swell reflected upside-
down in the bubble in the skull going by. link to link
      smile. piercing yelp of frustrated infant.

o

wood being fine, too, link, super-fine, following the
denier, the grain, gave me leave to love at last, link,
in a blue sky after rain birdsong to seem more clear
at last: that first small spider in the new house
its shadow, moving   dot   each plan plain. procumbent.
it would seem.

o

response: *look* – the whorled grooves of the seed-pellets,
meadowsweet.

o

…plant them.

RAIN

then cut this wood   with care   following its line
ply & tooth   the weapons are nothing   mind yr hand
keep time   cutting true & crude   then

tacked it   silver through yellow   a whole mountainside on fire

webshadow/masterstrand   affix, set by, scoop & try   shedding what
(little insect on a page) writing writhing riding
the waves' more basic music trebled, trembled   allows

& dreamtracing (the weapons are nothing) the array   a
light in the language   a light for the language
alighted in the dust of a hilltop village   the weapons   which

              is the flower you
              can grip this flower with
              extreme care

              once   are nothing

              clicks & ululations…

smoky homework of my students

hopeful homework of my students

the struggle in the homework of my students

the pathos in correcting the sad, smoky homework
of my students

              …big, braided rivers.

STEPS

a

driving in a red dustcloud
for hours years wandering
wondering how to

connect

this stone to that hut with
precision tact   two hands one
gift   wait listen   right
left   shimmering elastic

wallhome
(not any other barrier
 but a breeze over it)
welcoming.   conduit.

b

blue flower   strong stem
oval stone in a stream

I was stepping lightly home
(the baby developing)

starlings' jabber-click
cutting with the burin nick

conical hills   stone outcrop
two swans   one rooftop

dead flower   dead stem
dead stone in the stream

a fish shadows by. a cloud.
a bird. wake up, coward.

c

window lit
fire in the grate
door closed over
table set

food being ready
ready the appetite
(in dreams begin steadi-
ness) come, sit –

peeling a piece
of bark to get
the smell of
the tree feeding –

when threads mesh as they cross
over they sing to us.

this is how to live.

AISLING

salt
in sand &
a sand-

stone
boulder standing
beside a

sand-
dune where
marram

points
the way the wind
went

strong
long in the wind where
(closer)

shadows
skim, touch, cut
into

deeper
dark in which dark
Darkness

darkened…
hollows, pockets, echoes,
what

Perfect
is & *Rightness* &
Justice

(a
   Giant turning in his
   skin)

but
nothing accommodates
it, nothing

a game
of rule-changing,
finding

the fulcrum
enveloping slate &
brick

leaf &
bark & a broken tin, breathe
in, this too,

out, slit,
flower of surprising shocks,
growth-rings,

code messages,
strange processes in secret
underground

a flower
locked(in secret)underground
but

feeling
the pull of that nearby star…
this

vertical
pinprick pipsqueak –
Perception!

(possible
  states & possible
  combinations)

each
a gift a
burden

each –
prophecy, friendship,
finitude

wrapped
up in foolishness &
yearning –

seven
apertures, one
head.

RETICLE

Feel of the twigs in your
hands dry, dead, aromatic, that
passingness of/but the sides of this song
brush fire in it and kindle/slap
goes yr foot in the wet/slap/where
was I?/the/slap/tempo to honour the/
then rain/slap/fire/busy in the
world/slap/. A tripod in a bubble!
Slashed and bitten; clawed, hacked,
chopped. Tightened in the bud,
talisman, not an arrow telling
a narrow story, but/stamp/dash, splash
and/sound of money in the building
in the undergrowth/display. What?

o

A rat attracted by wheat in some
poison in the attic fell dead one
night behind where I sat. I was finishing a book; gathering kindling;
sleeping in a loft beside a glass-
covered gap in the gable, my window.
Politics. Afforested drumlin, ghost-
mist in the outwash.

This world is different, that one the
same. Patiently to disclose how little
you know, crow-echo in the chimney
flue, pet cricket. Step.

o

Cloudwisps connect. Correct. Crystals
lock a seed in. Correct. Smell of
nettles, water, watermint, willowsilver
in the air by the stream in the breeze,
clay, crushed grass-music, these take you
about and turn about together in their dreampool.
Correct. Flick and dazzle, the freedom to
move, step, the colours at the base, on site,
prior, primary, jigdance, write: fire

FIRE

fire
a quick breeze among
leaves pushes the
music lightly
into the visible &
through it out again
gone. forsythia begins:
a bright sudden *thanks*.
   here. (hand)   then
   up   there (wing)
   en   closed.
knows a
way. away
over
there.
over.
   in a flicker of
   stabs at that vast
   central column of
   (   )(being)
   (contacting zig-zag
    connecting verticals)
   (the air in the bones
    of the bird in flight)
   a miraculous access
   twists: once. &
   once. calling
   to each other in
   hedges & trees.
what's in the news then?
water in a river
in a circle at that point,
political. dark cell
old things
flat on your back
stone on your belly.

       imprint in the mud
          on the bank.
predawn whimper of a pump
in the dust.

FOUR CORNERS

PASTORAL
    Skin of the earth on
    earth   fragility

    agility
    profusion of bud-plans

    of   &
    blot manoeuvre corrode

    do I/we/you/they
    have to repeat even more
    more?

    It's
PASTORAL
    When grasslands disappear
    & the slopes are denuded

    topsoil
    without grip

…the finial pit
    of the first recorded

    raindrop

    bangs
    the tympanum.

    Let
PASTORAL
    Small wave-like motion of
    sound/someone singing

in a radio in a
kitchen over a

hedge on a windowledge
somewhere not far off.

Some bits
of words of
interest

or is it a
woman singing

outside the radio
her heart out?
PASTORAL
   Valleys, villages, coastline. A map
of a stain on a wall. Alive & living,
not a crammed glasshouse of pistillate
verba. Grass bends back. The book
is fat, contains code. The world,
the water planet. The code contained in
this thing in the world, the book, changes
the things, the world. Elytral sutures
open & wings, surprising & beautiful,
begin to work. The point is. Fernbrush,
nervure of such wings, small pebble
adjustments. Song.

IN THE MUSIC

Who's minting our tickets anyway?
I mean, looking back, an orchestral These-Which is what
    presents in this filter, yes?

Philosophy: tell me, is there a hole in the future?
Tell me, who sticks Advice to the webs?
Wait, I said (Choreography) wait a minute (delicate
    interconnected communities) is yr head yr home,
    the world a vigorous perianth of seven hundred billion
    teeth?

Tacit slap of underwater wave-fold, secret sub-shadows
    taking in the beat of the solar roar in yr ear where
    xenophilia built a commentary, the clouded leopard,
    bramble and grasses, smell of the green laneway in
    the summer rain, a fly hitting a windowpane. Click.
I let's see ah yes.

coda

RAIN

when I look at what's
I wonder dust between
the toes just branches
that don't catch/what
underlies what? a wrong
tack that but/stone leaf
air give back fumbling
along a path almost some-
times to con even yr
even yrself
talk to yr children
eye to eye
talk to yr children
not embargoes &
economic sanctions talk
to yr children wait
for what impact comes
from such (instar) such/
matted & black/fernhead,
nutrient moisture at
the grasstip the more
the most complete
stupidity globed. so. &
returns. sprung vertical
from the bud discutient
properties in gravel &
knots in the body
my little boy's first
tooth to go is so
small & perfect
ly tapered & white

there's birdsong & light
mint underfoot   sums.

spoon, chalk, cup. the empty
pocket & the raindrop.
down between ply, counterply
almost every edge's argument
holds. (or do they?)
(*seafóideach!*) jostle & equate.
big pencil in childfist.
that. just that.

RETICLE

A

Years ago one winter evening travelling
through Ireland on a bus I watched a
moon like money in the sky. (I dislike
similes, Mary, you know me.) The moon
was like money. Like money. Pulsing in
my breast-pocket, bright sterile dust-
rock, just like money. Circular shine
against black, a brilliant silver, crystals,
poison. A fine spray of chemicals in the
brain, that tree, this lake. Colours
on the flag ripple the wind still, that
dazzling spinning blue sphere in the dark.

Cold tonight. Paid the rent. Maybe a glint
from a passing car, a tempo gathering through
your life to here, and right to this point,
up to this point, still, still not for sale.
Provided that.

Your number please. Furry pod. Living in a
dream of news where information magnified to
a grainy blur … Made a few things, maybe a
few things, thought-gathering. At least the
pedant busy with his pedantry, but here
an ache of disciplined listenings over long
spaces, to make "a this" that is not for sale.

B

That box, that lamp, that bottle on the table.
You follow a path, eyes down, ears beginning –
the pursuit of healing – intricate alleyways
in crushed grass fibre under a stone,
bright ant-eggs, at least this pedant busy
with his pedantry, but here … music.
Clocks. A thousand buried years of not opening up
until something – heat and shock – oozes through.

C

Talking colours with my son – he's five, I'm
thirty-nine/he's right, I'm an idiot – the wren,
arrowtailed shadow in the hedgeplace, ready, each
crease in the hawthorn's argument, the leaves move.
Catch your foot in a hollow. Tap on a drum.

Tip scales: black sky, then rain. Flashes.
And this rain hammers out a drama on the ground
sending up steam and a loud roar on the tin roof
and a shiver up the spine. And someone is ringing
a bell in the village to hurry this angry spirit
on. Move on, move on. Kindle, kindling, kind, kin,
kine, K, the yellow, the red earth washing into
the dongas and away.

STEPS

    wake dreaming I mean you can
        wake up dreaming
    or dream living; what's that?
        branch-tap.

    bell rings, on the wind,
        & wavers & rings.
    a table & a Table-
        Waiting-for-Things

    through a chorus moving
        the song along to/but
    not for long, not for longing.
        feet on the ground

        yr feet on the ground
        out of the

              blue.

FIRE

A

suddenness of what snow does
to a doorstep when you
wake to it in the morning
early before almost anyone

(& why the verb *to be*
 in so many languages
 at such an angle should be
 so irregular so often)

a slate gone there
emphatic & there too
yes wind blew this way
not that when

(is a mystery to me.
 where were you when they
 named the name of money
 in your name anyway?)

& snow fell graphic many
ways across you (curls joinctures
loops stops) to make that black & white
unmelting music of what is

B

being coiled into a deft, modified past
not in money-work but secret
difficulties darkness pleated
dovetailing deeper dark down to
an all-dimensional ground blackness
being coiled into a deft, modified past
hollowing, carving, cutting (I went out.
I met nobody/I came back. faced it.)

the greedkeep, health, sanity, calmness where
the roots are, coiled, magnified,
crystal spindles at the branch-heads,
spasm of light

        a wind that
        turns a leaf on
        the ground or
        ientate
        yourself.
        -

        grey black
        stone ochre.
        grey black
        ochre clay.

        o

some monumental crap about gathering honey
in the tympanum of a bank's facade
small waterplanet tubby patriots
minim of "known" history vertical siphon, pip.
dogfish upriver, another world
light through glass touching the light
curtain reflected on a tabletop surface
upside-down repelled
returns –
pax! paxpax! pax!
goes the fighting in the street
being coiled into a deft, modified past.

        -

        grey black
        ochre stone
        grey black
        ochre clay

        o

C

a triangle of sun
light on a
wall of a
shed.
  blue sky. join the
  dots. child-wit.
  blue plane.
  the blue
  plane
draws the eye
along then
down to
chim
  neys & rooftops. here
  we are. slightly
  closer to the
  heart
of creation (but still
not close enough)
at the base of
an old tree
(minúte
  grains of white quartz
  imprint of the nail
  in the mud/the
  webbing bet-
  ween 3
toes & mare's tail sprung from ooze
a spider web, ready) a small
bird buried. even that.
the tune complifact
scraptured.
  five seagulls in V-form-
  ation & a quick
  sparrow too
  makin a
  mane.

it's wonderful to wake up sometimes
to a feeling of time in the morning
early, crisp, moving for a moment in
the first day always, clasp & bars
of the metal gate in the hedge outside
(say) by the pathway where – can do on
contact – the garden – you are – a glass
of cool water on a sunlit sill – in-
tricate tickle on the face – bright berry –
air puckered where the silkseed
drifts *that*

held to the Waiting Posture, *that* music an instant
fit to stave only an order in a sea of which/&
orders. when a token's taken & returned
fluent – "beautiful ideas for prov-
iding truth" – a *legal-decision-*
trial-peace pouch in waiting
(pat)

  clé deas
    you could ex-
 plain
        Peru
release the Trees
   Animals
       Engines
joining a
  Geometric Dance
on a shed wall
       of an evening
 vertical to the *why* in yr pockets
(otherwise empty you go about with
  proud & prim nonetheless)
 mirrors gaps branch-formations
 the very sight in the head –
   conical hills
   stone outcrops –
staving off all aggressive parasites

Steps

  & ear to the beat of breathing
  returned renewed & singing
     why
  /whirring pipsqueak/can't-thinking
   why can't thinking
    fit thinking fit
    this   apt
    black black
    grey red
    black red
    grey grey
     black

      o

Fire i.m.: Paul Klee

adherence

i: ABC

BALLAD

oo

Stop.

Walking through
leaves on a hilltop
was being will in

balance tell valency that
chance is a hand (step)
spread in the light, see

shade you don't
dread/thread where
you are/a long

time thing
shining
but

not a word

nervure of a fly's wings
to blur the lens, difficult,
working through, watching,

taking note, watching, puzzled,
delighted, in a presence
(never anything by rote)

beyond sense, sentient.
Black green
blue

all of the welkin well despite any
petty personal grouch under your
spreading canopy and –

pick an apple from a tree,
apologize –

like a bird
flit but

not a word

difficult. The broken
pieces, spoken
pieces,

fleet mother
of like-
ness

twisting a glass
in a tunnel

whisper-movements in the grass,
quill-scratch, trickle-piece
(click) but/The speed,

the light, the space. Even your next
conception of the. Height. Of a.
Glass wall stops.

Not it. No. Move … a long life and
a quick death brushed by the
rhythmic wash of the rain

the rule is the pieces to wait for
the right moment
the pieces

the echo-places where
smooth spaces
between

the eye of the net and the eye
waiting and taut
and

a love of watching a flower
matching the sun's face
following

a blackbird's silhouette on a last
branchtip, note-bits finely
mapping the place/but

– clouding, clearing, clouding –
does teaching *really*
exist?

– stop – stand back – let me see – not a word –

ripples slip across the
surface of the glassy
water where

a flat stone dropped from
its flight from
me

                to mark the spot in the lake
                    with precision
                        tact —

a shattering rain of
names
and

part-names beaten out of/eaten
out of meaning,
house, home

and that planned future
mortgaged to your
systematic

Friend at the Bank downtown as
the Furniture Beetle's
audible

rasp over your head under
your very nose
busy/but

not a word —

                    stopped

            ink to the paper dancing
            vanished thy besy praier
                  in speciall

                lift up your heart
                    and sing

*wingflash/finprint/loves-in-
the-storm/between
minūte*

*& brief, & back,
the leaf arguing with the light*

where the rock splits in a palace
of despair-places, shock
of mountain avens

taking my pen thinking to
put it down again
often

and pausing to having the real
eyes for and still not moving
a nearly not knowing yes

a lightning chrysalis

acrobatic
bright
cone

to the centre (infoliate,
quiet) of quietness, quietness
giving way to quietness

opening, entered,
spring/neap.

Drop.

°₀°

        Tree-
      touch, air-
    waves, leafmark.
  Step. A guide may be
indentations in the tree, if you
need a guide, a grip. Step. Not
ever again not any admonition or
any song. The term laid stark and
   the edges precipitous.
 Step. Which terror can you dare
   choose to ingest first? It all
   could be worse. *La vitesse* in life,
L'espace in hope of peace in place
and your life placed at the
border and the border de-
fined. Step. To the
  top, fluent, and
    from there, to
      begin.

I had a pot of white paint on a red ladder
and was painting a kitchen window
in a cool breeze on the last day of May.
Slight pain in the head. Glancing at a fly
on a wall. Birthday, for emphasis. Fact:
to dislike the walls of the cave. Stuck.
Fact: cool breeze. Fact: old red shirt.
Hop on your bike and fix your fyke, keeping

each new silly surface clean beside a
breeze-block wall, a game of boxes in the
Late Upper Holocene. First the small one for
the narrow edge. Then the wide one for the beam.
Dip. Fact: where one stone touching another
stone in the dark in silence in a tower where
lichen spreads at its own speed on the light-side
and a spiral staircase won't stop going up.
Stop. Stone. I'm not/or/I'm waiting in that
space where Black keeps eating White,
a philosophy of craving, a trick the reaper
likes repeating – pliant tube, tufted frond –
a way into this delicate fossil-music,
dark, light, indigo, coral, that won't leave
my daren't my ear alone. Life is. Ever more
briefly, bright. Sit. Giggle-blather. Tell
             nobody. Dip.

Rest, happiness, peace in discipline
take water for instance a passerby
stopping for music & good food yes
the sound of the water the river but
that which can't be described.

A fly cleaning itself precisely
by a window in sunlight
forelegs back (rest) head eyes
shadows wings brittle-quick & quite
like writing really. Out there. That.

---

of every person who would be a party to
a conveyance to the fee simple free from encumbrances
of the property described in the schedule hereto attached
buzzed the/flash/by the glass disappearing sideways
into a or in the direction of

> at least a
> pentad of
> *(on top of*
> *the world*
> *air thins*
> *out & heaven*
> *laughs)* trees

Rest happiness peace old
pain-in-the-head (mica-fleck,
cricket-click, a black & white
flash, five-fingered flower on
a cave wall) vanishing &
glinting in the triple breeze.

Intricate walking (happiness)
down a laneway with the twins
small house – by a river –
lesser celandine, wild strawberry
in flower. Just love. Nobody wins.

Your wooden ladder of *As If* to play with. *Hah!*
Actinic. Up the steps. One one one one one.
That circle of coincidence that brought you
here from Africa to capture tourist brochures
of the soul for a season for a song that.
Don't look back. Or

down. The ant moves a grain. The ant disappears
underground to come back again with a grain.
The ant moves the grain then disappears underground
again to get another grain to build and/click/
it goes down there through other into the dark
to get more and. Grains allow themselves to
be touched. Slap. Touched by elaborations for
what archaic quillities, the code, the children
giggling by the river, duck, past, gone, clarity
holding the sky (bridge) up holding the sky up, too
(stone). One one one one one.

Down
goes the machine down
through the steel chute
black diagonal shadows
marking a regular pattern pacing
its controlled descent with a whirr
and a click as – down – close your eyes –
pip goes a car in the street far – as may be –
away *pip-pip* in response meaning: The World
is all that is in phase – meaning: – down –
The eare is a rational sence – down – and
certain – meaning: a chiefe judge of proporcioun

                too

adding (down) leaning to the law that
each thing its number its place
between the/*because* of these shadows
interlocked and separated figures
things missing or things wedged side-
ways that remind us that all orders
have their justification in the end in
an order of orders only our faith as
we work, addresses – oh! –
slows down and stops to lock level with a
click: door-grid slides back…

    Dust rising from the track
    where the dance started
    in the heat, concentrating each
    tap on the tympanum,
    travelling elsewhere how
    shadowbits, lightsplashes –
    pick an apple from a tree –
    a door, a desk, a window,
    a crude thing for anyone
    to hide in over the years
          maybe…

This thing about understanding. *(Ah.)*
Not a machine of measurement. Not:
a flower. If, hemmed in. The core
body is/shouting in the street?
Fruit a spherical berry, scarlet.
Streetlights spear a pool. It
would appear. A pollen sequence can
take you back fast and yare. Clearly.
This thing about poetry is

    or it might not quite
    be what you said is what
    the map you said you had
    set out to say – aim straight,
    fire wild – you thought I was
    (and I was you) blunt, stark,
    mysterious. *What?*
    Rough but ready
    states yes your steady
    hands made of contact
    sweetness, white traces
    in snow-charred crystals
    as secrets, geodes.
    Let a leading shoot
    be a landing place:

        poor, human, stung.

It is the end of June.
Swallows and a grey sky.
Are we entitled. To the
ripple where a stone drops.
This is the ripe cone
after the seed is shed.
Ash, feathery leaf-light
shadow and half-
shadow mind-breath, sacred.
It could be the beginning
of September or maybe

the middle of March I'm
in the tropics suddenly
inside the arctic circle not
dizzy but waiting to bloom…

o

The leading shoot
is the land-
ing place.

ii: cohering

Sudden Glory

SETTING

Look
it entered a shed
through a
crack under a
closed door
following then
sending up
sun-hungry leaf
for life to vie
till it found
well nothing
particular to
grow around so
turned(look)back.
To the sun. Settled.
All those books
& nowhere to go?
"Yr life will be
full of happiness
(marks in snow
　show snow-negatives
　in grey-white
　blackwhite) happiness"
say the Bones. I see.
Pens, blue then
red. Bind
bound bindweed
found wine-seed
lime green
life-road twined
in triple flight
to fall to land
ground-side up,
under the sun.
Young pup
that you've

            always been
            prefiguring
            a print
            in a rock
            the print.
            The rock. Knock.
            Whether it wither
            in this weather
        or not, going back
              against the
                    books
            the dance of rain
            snow   discovery
            taking in   letting
            go   molecular pavanes
            in rings & chains
               pistons   combustion
            reading   doubt
                day/night chequerwork
            cloud-dance   tidal-
            dance   dance of the whale
               ants & bees   dance
            of the binary
            systems   dance of
            regenerating
            lithosphere   things
            in relation   rippling
            wing-edges
            dance of energy
            dance of the
            blood
                  the dance
            of the
                  blood
            slow sets
               shimmering nets
            mountains
               moving.
                  So.

Open the door,
step in, wipe feet,
leave the mat,
walk to the chair

by the desk, switch
on the lamp & the
heater for a bit too,
sit down, start.

Everybody's busy,
en route, clickity-clack,
but what you have
in your cave

one slim green
    arrow
my hands bare
filicoid stellate

waterpieces that
diffuse to the
surface wait
the chip-glint

in the rock that
cuts through cuts
through cuts
    despair

bird all-forgetting bird designate bird shimmering
    Despair.

There is a cold solar haze. There is smoke.
And blue. And gold. Emphatic branchtangles,
angles of (Victorian) chimneypots, rails,
wires, traffic, the pouring canal by Newcomen
Bridge. An impossible accent placed in gay paint
there over the P in *Oifig an Phoist* by
Newcomen Bridge. *Éist! Éist liom!* Ghostlanguages
of herofurniture. Even here, dipping into
yr bag, lips pursed, eyebrows raised, sound of
the guttural morse of the swallow.

I was crossing a street when it struck me
suddenly – lights changed red – it came from
a wave from one of my books into Mountjoy Square
where the air was rolling back in front of it.
(Daddy, Daddy what's yr book?) (Oh that the
anthropoid's too fussy today we can't but agree:
I love myself & you love me. But I so love
another for her delicate grace I can't peel my
bananas or pick the nits from yr face.) Set
Thing Ring Net. The twig snaps. Waters that/that
fatten to an icicle. Echo of axe coming down
on wood – pale bole, dark ground – under whose
shade the ant takes a grain, the replicate grain
tapped in – smart, accurate – below ground.
Palp. Here I am. Peace is a small house by a river.
Sound of the water. A cobweb in yr doorjamb
in the morning after dew. Splits the world in
rainpools ... Daddy? I made a song in a murderous
time. Listen to the sound of that.

AND DESPAIR

A quiet
chipping draws
my attention back
to my window where
the laws of tension
The poetry of despair
is blank. Sit. Quote.
Birds fly, tie down
the birds. Mind darkens,
rock splits, head
blazing, hands hope-
less in place of
splinters where the laws
of listening & the laws
of tension meet
the laws of light…
to fight it out
in whispers.

    listeners there
      are &
  steady hey but

    cohere? go there
look: hanker after
    people or a

    god or a blinding
      pattern
    one of the

    smallest birds in
the world its
    nest the size

    of half a
      walnut shell
    built to such

    deft such delicate
these feathers
    leaves even telltale

    flower-petals moss
      hair feet
    bill spider-thread

    weaving or the
bird's own saliva
    together or both

    dancing in despite of even

      .   out over
      mimosa flicker past
      the village to
      the mountains

their eggs even
  their eggs themselves
stuck down fast

against gales one
flat yes precision

   stuck down
      fast

   oo

Good. To have invented
happiness. To have to
re-invent it

under stress. Sit down
stand back/filament
filament

feathery the web in the flue that's
held this house up for
so long for

you for instance so
pliant so desper-
ate

so long the
smoke
says

(fringed with mystery just
 beyond the splash
 zone)

so long
as I
can

(*now* I
 know
 oh)

tiny multiple
rivetings
I

(can't quite/Love
 as a garden
 escape?)

(dog in a hurry leg up
 tail erect off again
 busy) quite

grip it/the shaking shadows
of the dead when
sifted/

that plastic bag that
spits & whispers in
the breeze

"...*Spirit?* What do *you* know
 about poverty
 of spirit

 anyway? For comfort & luxury
 a cinch to swindle a
 lyric poet or two

(for instance) with a vulnerable
brother to boot for
instance

when the strong players die
get senile or otherwise
out of the way

& dice collide. Listen.
Listen just slip into
action within a day

or so of burial pretending
caritas-loving-concern
to the place where

hinges singe & the money burns
& hey presto. Lick, twist.
The light. Ethical?

Rubbish! This is how it works, this
is Life spinning on its
radical pretence:

an old bone in every family – the Weak
shall inherit the Dearth, the
shadows. Surely you know

that? Stand back.
Gouging pretty
messages

on the Church-Bank door –
there goes Michael
rowing his

bloody boat ashore again & good
riddance (Alleluia) – now
that I think of it

is yr cup of tea, isn't it?
Delicate-
ness

art & significance
& all that.
Get a job.

I just thought I'd pass it on
for what it's worth sonny,
a little bit of light

on embezzlement & misery.
You don't get the
picture? Then

    don't be *in* it.
    Stand back…"

Oh

the Cockatrice Greed-in-Life Rampant
Gules.

Good.

Pasture. Sky. Bird.
Time to go. Time-time.
Some sound. Sound-sound.
Steps. A wall. Sun. Instar.

Barred bead along a string
(call) continuing meets a
stopped bead at the other side to

/tick/should it/might it/but…
Counts. Then nouns then verbs. Sit.
     Are.

    Bright sun bright
    white wall fine
    flowerhead blazing
    red. Tally. Bright.

    Sun bits. Blue light.
    Green butterfly. Gold
    pupa. Shadow-
    sound. Oh right.

        Cut
        through
        that
        too

TO THE

Ten thousand
intent at desk the
in stopped swirl
the ten thousand
things that convene
shine escape
intermittent material
in a pipe that
& that dying out. Half
a walnut
a shell.

Whereat the root
music of the unpat
threads means to/
then but/

CUT

Alive to the slapped silver & black
water & sunlight a lime tree twig
versatile against gales gone into the
upper layer & stuck down fast in a fault
in the mind in need of repair even leaves
that angle back to listen to the beginning,
harmonies bathèd in charm in a cave
somewhere, cohere. To stick down fast
one flat, yes, precision.

Let's see: glue to the web. *Cast yr nets
before the jelly sets.* Be prepared.
Don't despair. *It's a tradition, bits of
attrition.* Short breaths, in small space,
second thoughts, first steps, in April
& replete, begin. Forget. *A web is a
crowd of kisses.* Ah. Chuckle in the locks.

A ballad, knocked flat, someone in yr
memory, frantic to be back. Forward: dis-
appear into a multiple glint of twisting
arabesque (with point). Up: blank. Down:
blank. To the sides: blank. Alive & breathing
– swim, reptile!

SMILE

Sudden Glory
is the passion
which maketh
those
Grimaces
called LAUGHTER.*

Ever. And ever after.

*Thomas Hobbes

THE GEOMETRY OF SOAP BUBBLES

A hot cuppa in a cold shed, a wintry blast
outside & far away in Endwhile unbelievable
rumours of peace among the nectar suckets…

        o

only a few rules & those/to pick
a step here a thumbprint there
to twist it into pieces until
crystal specifics splinter against
          chary when given what might be
          what/bulloney (the key?)…
got a job mornings setting up oilcans
governed by a few elementary
weighty five litre cans in navy
silver screwcaps three pyramids on
three pumps
          & two as proud under the window
          ESSO – yes O/*they can form are*
          governed by the few the rules
          my hands *can be shown*
the till had a moneysmell
to be self-healing with respect to
small punctures paper & sweat I suppose
& continued Living too edge to edge
the locks(no)still can't click(pert)open
          or just watching laburnum flare
          & snow on the lawn opposite (who can
          tell what it is explores a madness
          in a man Mary anyway hey & you know
          me) stuck in this honeycomb scribbling
          away
pawning the bloody typewriter again
& a few other Elementaries borrowed

for the occasion *the geometry*
of the possible the blurred vertigo
the quick breathing the special pleading
& still patch
                Monday to Friday putting in the
                weddingring & the iron given the
                sensibility to receive them as
                lights change red yr number please
                (dog sniffing wet stain on back
                tyre of hearse) (empty glinting
                exoskeletons in multiple traps
                in the grass *tinkling* in a light
                vast trawl-sock)
& run out of busfare too a dab
at borrowing by this time *can come*
together despite *in only two ways*
knowing well the rules that
equalled the incapacity to move
through configurations yr friends
extend in yr regard with
                love flash of tail-feathers
                (scribbling) downright-fangled
                Love O it was a happy life
/chary/or care fernlike
starlike *The possible*
configurations governed
by a few elementary rules
that have been
                known for more than a
                century. This new mathematical
                model provides a sound
basis for those rules.
A sound basis for those
rules. Sudden glory.
Blueprints as to use
on the walls
                of caves, the makers' instructions'
                magic: magic still, splinters that
                light a winter window echo

echo the little finger,
ring, middle, index,
knucklejoints, thumb, palm,
wrist, deep in the world,
open, touching.
        Look.

The possible configurations they can form are governed by a few elementary rules that have been known for more than a century. A new mathematical model provides a sound basis for those rules etc

from THE GEOMETRY OF SOAP FILMS & SOAP BUBBLES
by F. J. Almgren Jr & J. E. Taylor (*Scientific American*, July, 1979)

iii: DEF

LULLABY

Yr father blank in a chair.
Bored tired deaf blind dirty.
Nurse calls in to the wrong ear.
Alert but not sure of the year.

Yr friend soaks a relative for money
yr brother terrified cuts & runs
yr wife yr children yr body ageing
bored tired deaf blind/damn it/all of these things –

        sanity phones
        listen this that
        rubbish & bones
        life is hate –

sit down then to concentrate this
hopelessness into an art that's
locked in to the point where a
key clicks yes but heart sinks –
bored tired deaf blind – down to all
        these all of these all

of these things piled up to here do
you hear can you hear me me falling too
father yr head against the wall-wall
of yr room cracks with a bang & jammed
against the piano & the door I can't
        get in

to you until we find the key to
life is easy isn't it piling up the past
in the mist deaf blind it ever occur
to you among world-things to look to
the place where the money screams then

			blind deaf then
			   it's over
			    over?

		    Rubbish & bones
		     listen my love
		     listen to this
		     pass it on.

I was a boy once, then a young man; now in middle age, both;
(each edge of each allegory twining the spine of the rentbook).
To fool a trout, Blue Lulu. To fool me, a peck of honesty.

RSVP

Picked a flowerspike
then to look at what
love gives to found things

the world gives up cast
ing nectar for your
passing

(comes-goes on a chance
wind and a dance then)

as you go goading
the vagaries they
like to call

(dances back a bark-
er on a loudspeaker)

thinking no thinking
at all there though really
after all but stormed

out anyway to fix a bicycle
& pedal about.
It was dead.

Quite.

And you were singing.
Lyrics! Iridescent
ly pressing the point

into empty entries
in the back of
the Book of Love:
scraps, glints, cries…

Welcome to paradise!
Kicking the chrysalis
(from the inside)
a house a prison

to trap a woman in
or a delight of
connected spaces
(what do you think?)

to live in. Well
then.

The branch the air
is our life
together if
not this then never

hope to be open
to pass this gift on
to our children
in place of

a block of
locked in
ungrowth fake
love. Lack. Unmake

then remake to last
at last to the last
on the last the flash
the river the fruit.

The river the silt.
The river the trace.
That ache at the per-

imeter fence yours ours
yes but this love
travels.

Thinking a notebook hers she found instead masses of her husband's work in it – touch a web, send a message: Ballad of the Bumble & the Bee, Fact, Bract & Root-Bit stuck fast in a crumpled chorus, locked out, leaking in. Flick pages. Stark place briefly visited between bewilderments the simples difficult. Do. And difficulties gather in shadows – nosong, reednib/ filicoid, stellate – one seed and that one ready…

STEADY

To continue taking in/ingesting
World as a Dancing Column of Light
doesn't tally at all with your pretence
of not noticing the inside of the bucket
HEY! I'm *Talking* again not dancing
I thought I said disclosing <u>Instructions</u>
enclosing exposing FLASH

Gathering with the forelegs, moving pizzicato,
crouching, shrinking, stabbing, sticking, dis-
appearing into a crevice, or down a silk tube
[*exuding (over) the visible / intruding (on) the
visible / eating the leaves leaving only/*]white,
grasses, thickets, exhibiting drops of dew, in
very x-ray, wall-corners, ceilings, windowpanes,
doorways. Sharpen your pencil and begin again.
Dead men, dead men draw me into line, mud villages,
blue skies: squint, sharpen the eyes, where women
carry everything…

And then I woke up. It was early. I was
in a shed in a garden in spring, snow
melting from roof and branches, a cock
robin foraging under a hedge and I knew
…I knew it was time to open my notebooks
again with a clear mind and a long memory
and make a start. Testing.

---

*If I sat quite still a squirrel would come up
and pick a berry, turn it over, detach a
section, one at a time, eye me, brightly, then
eat it. The small sweet seed. A meticulous
performance. In this painting Gepetto is hoping
to get on with his own life, apt and drab,
presentable obsessions with a good shelf-life.
Speak to me. Yes I'm an artist. The lilac-breasted
roller, the malachite sunbird. Listen… Then
a second cat along a rooftop stops.*

TESTING

Pang goes a particular raindrop
in a plastic bucket under a tree.
Now. Which do you prefer & which
is your favourite leaf in that
particular preference-tree anyway?
(Shadow-light)+(shadow-light), skid-
dart go the swallows, dab, gouge,
the wedge in the clay///twenty-three

(look) triangles in a drawing my
daughter made for me years ago
look back at us/you now in middle
      age – stiff, lost, sad:
when the dance changes the world
      changes the dance

changes the dance changes: broken
bits make a mosaic, mosaic a
picture, picture a blur falling
into darkness, darkness folded on
darkness, old places shot through
multiple veins of new surfaces
in old places: Peace – Happiness –
under a lion's paw under a furnace

    under the sun.

·

---

pang

coda

Hey-you! goes the train on the line
setting & abetting
clack-at-a-click

turning on its stem
the Then &
the Far

one two
one three four
two

touched suddenly
suddenly a smell of wet leaves
on wet grass

under black trees
in early winter
when/one two

one three four
two/what you
get is

grain of the present
in the light presence of
a tensed

stone skipping
              wrinkles
on the water-surface
still
    (tapped)

a Man not a dog-on-a-lead
for the moment anyway un-
sure which of us be dead

slips past sideways
now that I understand
dabbing I think

bright blurs &
out again the other
side

in flight/benign scar
just over the (there)
hawthorn tree.

In. Maurice Scully is dead.
Long live
light

(postcards from Paradise –
chewing gum – interviews – all
that – yes)

hand on
the page & the pen
moving

sun going down
& the moon shining over
cowshit

& a cracked look & a cackle
echoing & I sit down
to write

listen/listen to it/listen
bright berry/pale flower
needle-shadowy

nets
of
preparatory conditions

that underpin
that abc
you get when

dog-eared on your desk in the dogged
bogged down
pursuit of the sweet

you speak
spitting T-squares &
callipers

patter
cut out of the pattern
& a seed ready

growth-lines gravity-tracks
seaprint in the
grain

cluck-thock
of water under a caried
rock/dark

the little falsities let go by
till the garble
mountains/

seed ready
cone doubled
cry out

a
lifetime's
work

cry out cry out cry out
sapwood testing its liquids
& the shadow-spirits

in the street
in a split second too/cut/
into you.

postlude

FORGETTING EVERYTHING

i

Or that wearing repetition of
children – towards you/or
for a long time

crushing
vividness.

Or certainly fevered delusion
but look my health's been
bad these weeks

& again *yes* this reptilian slyness
for instance in press
photos or:

in itself nothing – but
or: sliding
down

the middle of a well-greased
chute/or: punctures the
limits of mere

   steel
    grey
    grey
      sky

taps sunlight circles &
hits glass arrows
clicks slaps

incised & illuminates blues
& golds & a 1,000
flowers &

    travels through

cleats – veins – frets – combine
& mingle – brittle
crazie

cool in here nel duomo
& for tourists?
<u>history</u> duecento lire.

And then
she suggested
this way.

We won't do that
again she said
one-two

wobbling finely – mirror
tilted – so that
that

something lodges
obdurately (in
the net)

tilted – cool in
here – in
history.

Or.

But how can you write about emotion
when you forget everything
the next day.

VARIATIONS

Once upon a time there were three
billion bears. Ling. Dab.
Who studies happiness

now – busy crazy – who? An ABC
of Letting Go lets go – oh
look – or

deaf to the what-in-what – stunned/
back from hospital
on our way back

too back to the wall
my old dead
father

summer to winter to
beginning-spring/
cut.

A fist tightened of a
sudden forgetting
itself

opens – glint in the windowpane –
morning – cloudless –
sunlight –

a gull on a chimneypot –
dog in a
garden…

but to spend the time just so
dust in a
laneway

shadows across
birdsong
(bus

  en route) falling floating-
falling
their

mesh diagonal over
surfaces that
tilt black

ribbons into dark green pools then
wait – answer – expand the
view: Tuesday/sharp.

What you need here are millions of precise steel tools.
[p 255]

At the Question-Wall though at the heart of
the Lattice/Oh let me be
faithful to

your humble among your
polysnobberies
(otherweb

  elsewhere take
  over take
  cover)

– translate then scuff
  yr slate &
  play –

busy crazy too & so my heart
in the constricted thing
(stung) o saisons o châteaux

the petty business of freedom
the solo the
hopeless

& no end to that wriggle of the mind &
no relief whatever anywhere ever
to be had.

So. Born to be slaves & monkeys forever?

I'll go down among people on foot
tonight/bees in the plum blossoms
busy crazy/

gag that pack-of-dogs thinking
in my head trapped &
travelling in

isolation here/to get to the
temple hot with its punctual
flock   (cut granite)

to get to the company of those never
practising freedom never
or isolation

pen   creel   hive
fire   ice   or
to   yes

you me everybody
each *isola*
SPACE

I parted my hands to refocus
took pen from jacket
& began to

write down some noises
I thought I could
hear a leaf

make falling hitting
those other
branches

angl-
ed twist-
ing

in its canopy in
transit to land
on my page-

top here on my table-top
bid bead bed bod then/
then delete that oh

just another born-again
quietist waiting to
bite back. But

no. Check the micro-
scope. What? Iris
& lilac.

Wait a minute I only want
six sections with a break at
five & the insertion of this
here would make a seventh in
total &/rest happiness peace/

You me everybody
each *isola*
aching

waking up to/in
desolation in
a grey

nothing of nothing
(touch me) noting
& (dot)

doting over this tight co-woven
anti-original
half-

thing/iris & lilac
busy & crazy. Who studies
happiness now?

Split. So.
Decided.
Together

dotdot wrapped up in
themselves &
about to/

happiness? Back to
the wall. I'll
go down

tonight shedding shredding
the personal
rubbish

that
clung
so

O now I wouldn't do that.

Tiny
temple-silhouette –
crisp serrations –

barely visible. If you look up
do you see heaven?
Once

upon a time. Cling to the
rung. Don't look
down

(to how many teddybears
 having how much fun
 anyway?)

tree-shimmer tree-towering tree-whisper
tree-cold that shapes &
holds – don't –

in the/it's a destroying fire   a supralucent
liquid   there   if   either   then
but   definitely

four children two adults under a plane tree
in the rain suddenly –
mine – bare –

network of billions of microscopic
delicate precise
dots

in the dance
improvised
& manic

that fits this magnetic lock's
secret internal
crease &

is sucked
into
its

slit/quick/the key
& dissolved
in a hiss

of acidic steam – the sky/sparrows
busy in the clematis on the
wall/

who studies
happiness
now

needles tickle the vacancy
plum blossoms   bees
busy & crazy

sprinkle water/mutter-murmur for solace
happiness   where was I?   stunned
back   o yes

to wet fingers/dance/before entering
& leave before the end of
ceremonies.

ooo

To
honour
the light
on the
pool the
rain made
on a foot-
path without
a sound
last night
hardly a
sound a
lightness
outside a
window out
of the blue
flower the
mind is
(too) then
/what must
we do?/
then *yes*
a: b: c:
touch taste
this is
the lifespan
spread on
a windowpane
glisten-spirit
back &
forth back
& forth
across
fields to
the hospital
under the
trees whose
pods underfoot
brittle in

grass as
you tackle
the echo
ing/the
hard-nosed
hard-eyed
hard-necked
hard-hearted/
dead-dead
it said
a Crow
loud into
an incinerator/
hang up
Sanity evap-
orate Death/
  touched.
  Touched
  suddenly
  suddenly
   awake.

o

KEY

I put my pen down
on paper
on a table
on a blank where

rubbish gluts the
tank/But/If/
Maybe/Or

blazing on yr graveside
beside complication bleed-
ing into complic-
ation & slick

the junction where
you think to stick points
round a true border
to/happy to give thanks

happy to know how
(to) happy to know
happy happy
not to also

solid radiant basis
where was I?
what date's today
this morning anyway?

acrobatic
bright
cone

>   mind open
>   mind able
>   if shadows pen
>   you in, cradle
>   you
>
>   where once you
>   stood/twice despair
>   rose –
>   *gasp* –
>   descending again
>
>   into helpless-hood
>   re-entering yr head
>   (recovered?)
>   coat on a table
>
>   open the water
>   open the fable
>   open
>
>   (from one rooftop to the other
>   side – drift – over the street
>   there a seagull as silently as that…)
>
>   yr life, lifting,
>   open.

                            oo

Call it a ballad because a ballad tells a story, the
story of a stone, mind skittering, touching/jumping
across a water-surface. Morning. Early. A thread of
prose in the weave just to keep you on your toes, children
coughing, jacket damp, air cold. Thirty items on a
three-page set mark the close of the five-book dance.

Flickering through my dictionary to check it I thought
yes – gone in a flash – yes/the door open: "Listen for
its song then try to spot one."

oo

At last doing these steps in reverse, it worked: No, no I know
quite well where I'm going, thanks ... *bang!* into a wall. What is
an assertion anyway? A landlord sucking rentals from the poor!
Down tunnels confused by, not enlightened by sporadic flashes, a
small pile of cut cardboard shreds, a lump of black plastic, a stapler
on its side, point of palmleaf, buckled flimsy, the merest threads

holding "stability" together.
Yes.

iii

The tree beside
the water's
standing

still – the water there
is standing too or
seeming to

though full of little dark
& darting things
& fluctuant.

The bird is in the tree
wind its briefly
on a branch

beside a leaf I see
twice then flies
back

over the ranch
to the
cliff.

The farmer is walking
across the dust
of the ranch.

Ridged bootmarks
in the dust of
the ranch.

The sky of this place
is blue. And justly
famous.

One two. An envelope of
useful chemical
reactions.

Cut down too on yr
tobacco intake.
One four.

Reaches his landrover. The Tree.
The Stream. The Bird.
The Cliff.

Water moving by in the stream
here has many fine
characteristics.

Look. Bird reaches cliff.
Fenugreek folding its
leaves

around its wedge-flower.
Lebanese?
Sundown.

Moonlight.

Living in a world where
things happen
someone

will play the viola
someone will &
someone

will & – counting
on it – a
large

crimson spider – a
small silver
gimmick.

Tearshaped apple-
seed moist
mahogany –

one two four/one
two four
three –

presence & pressure
of space – one's
future –

boundless periods of stillness
curling gradually
so that

each dream congruent
into the next
continuing

solo in shadows under
leaves out of the
sun in Sleepy Hollow.

Intricate mist building
on a window-
pane.

Four kittens lap milk
from a tray on
the ground.

Four apples in a
row on a
windowsill.

Arithmetic (Plato) *has a
very elevating
effect.*

Sonata

In Swahili *nyumba* means back and *mbele* front but for Swahili speakers the front of an object is its far side, facing *away* from the speaker, and the *nyumba* is the side facing the speaker.

I

...the money I can see
 from here
landing on the floor
 emitting little words
is not for me
 [where's my home?
how house
 my children?]
& when breezes shake
 the leaves a little
they all fall over
 into another country
evenly speaking
 Utopian-Glass-Box.
oh I'll be there –
 mouth wide –
interpreting off-key...

 then I woke up.

moving from the small
 stinking hotel
arranged for us by
 the school & too
expensive anyway
 to what turned out
to be some sort of
 brothel & then on
a few days later
 on his insistence
to a colleague's place.
 & his collapsing
marriage.
 drunkenness. fights.
a television
 flung to the floor.

we'd arrived – yes –
 but not quite yet

to that distant spot of
    sunlight where to
disport our wings over
    a forest floor.

    …space – air –
scattering influence
    over us – a
matter of discussion –
    doubt + idiocy
join the club –
    a split stone
in the storm/
    black white/
it glints & (click)
    purrs (of) yr
properties' keys
    in my pockets
index of what you
    think & what
you think is
    yours by right –
not omitting
    that niggling
ever-present
    fever to survive –
rain of dishonest
    badgerings
incessant valley
    of darkness –
it dissolves
    love blurs
at the edges
    gestelted thalurbs
overolve in the
    deep blue sea (will
I begin it?) the world.
    (that's all that's in it:
blue veins/pink

vines) then what?
gis a job – & so –
   down. (earth)
        that.
land on it.
    ignition –
back to the crannóg
   for me…

the angle of
the neck the
angle of the
bill the angle

& elevation of
the body the
ruffling of the
feathers on its

back & the di
   splay of
     the tail.

    pipe
        pip
    curl
        rill.

    swirl.
        sculpt.
    split.

dofheicthe
      in braille…

If you open a door & light hits the light on the floor
but doesn't double it or fit.   If you respond to her special
look & then it.   If a door closes gently its tongue clicks
shut ("shut") under-echoing along a hallway *shut*.   If you
wake in the morning overjoyed before a tide of worries in the
dark.   If the smell of rain in the air brings rain.   If the
Seamstresses of Steel become home-makers or widows at their
windows at home in chrome & leatherette.   If a war begins
& then stops & then begins again money & blood pouring through
– phase by phase – in gouts of/hey wait a minute –   If peace
is a gap within a gap.   If a painting falls to the floor –
then … then …   //It should be called Cascade – ode sac –
aubade – a glint of silver in a storm then gone. Dwell. Fall.
Time. Crushed butterflies. Tapping animal in a tree.

Tell that to the police.

This is the world.

Ah.

Your screen says no, says yes, says progress this way, no wait,
that … each problem yielding a new exfoliation of information
itself ready to burst into further layers & those layers further
… Tired, a sore throat. Tell me, tell me sweetly: I had
melodies, then maladies – was it Xmas? – & accurate pieces of
language. Pip-pip. Yes, it is a blackbird across yr neighbourhood
that calls, & then calls. A child's voice, a child's mind
("Will my brain *rot* when I'm asleep?")

       whispery verticals stab-slits tubular vivids
         draw past skin cheeks knuckles o
           must be in my other jacket
             sshish go cars on
               wet streets
           recuperating a blank
          below the moon device or
      something like & obliquity in water
     outside the calyx *touch teach touch* staying
put my house collapsing cards on contact reaches home.

Ode sac – aubade – a glint of wisdom against the norm then gone. Less than no use. In that frame. (*Hi, I'm Miró, wing-commander Miró, haven't we met?*) On the other hand, you turn to her for an explanation, & seem to get the beginning of it. A Japanese basket peddler pulling his laden cart (a century ago) dwarfed by the enormity of the contraption, intent under his conical woven hat: *that's you!* she says, & laughs. On the other hand…

                       O   O   O

the figure
I can see from here
is pegging wet underwear
to a line for drying
in the no-wind of the season
in this naïve painting clean
& warm/ing to ward off the inside/
outside good & god was taking notes

I felt
            yes these things are
animals in that ground the sky
but no wait much higher
& more powerful & faster.
that's a/a pretty mark. jet. the
deity. a machine. the deity was
inventing conspicuous beauty.
praise him. & his mother.

& it's hopeless. scuffs. shreds.
but: flick through the detours
abc of ornateness depth
without tears. that thing's not
alive it's a house. those things
in it are doors & windows to go
in & look out. & from your
shopping-list in the bottle?

fear. that's my green pen. that's
my job. please a little quicker because
I am in a hurry. how much? keep
the change. stand back. please
I would like to have my hair
shampooed too. please I would
like a massage. mind my moustache.
stand back. I am a merchant.

are you a manufacturer? I am
interested in yr goods. lattice-
patch. odes epodes ads.
*le seinm na gcuach ar bhruach
na gcoille go sámh.* my previous order
was not executed exactly. give me
a French coffee please. that's good.
have you jams?

objects in mirror
are closer than
they appear

is printed on my wing
mirror in white ink
& moves over what
appears there
     moving

          crest & swoop

     a playing mantis

  a host of golden
      raffle-tickets

    pinkish dust
    landing different
    ways around white –
    stylus to palmleaf –

    this is the life.

  (had it ever will be)

      +

(I'll was wont sought possible)

      =

  (the wallpaper)
if only we could see
    reason.

working in a corner at her desk.
let's discuss this more than/she
did say/dancing on the water-paper
surface – & – in full flight ... ah!/
a book – notebooks opening – the
concentric circles bedded in the
flowerhead. will get you a career.
next please. thank you. move along.
& it's a great laugh howling for
Injustice in the Land of the Golden
Treasury. piano-ripple from a kitchen
window over a wall. so be it/she did
say in Kikuyu no word for *thank you*
a thing given is given so what each
arriving lie gathered undiscussed
vertical to the centre of gravity
tubes bars rods a stirrup in bight
to minimize damage/fit the cup's
lip to yr lip so that you know you're
not dead. pay the bills. close the door.
don't break the surface don't shuffle
the pack. just stand back. each grass-
blade tilts either this way or that
from its tether. I've been around.
dent, pock. then something else happens.
Goodie-Two-Shoes. it's yr duty. it is
not. circles meanders blunders into a
lamp the fly hits my head. seeds shiver
then settle, a sound a comma makes
being made, that message of discomfort
in yr lower back (I mean lower soul)
not this ferocious rain-drama of the
tropics slamming onto my one tin roof.
& then went down to the ship. (& put
my hands in my pockets)

multiple gold-black bars
                dis/reappearing
  in clear
                      blue-green
    under a network
                        of small disparate water-
     flashes past a ferry

          is that a haiku?

      dancing
          singing
      & playing musical instruments.
            writing & drawing.
      tattooing.
            adorning an idol
      with rice & flowers.
            colouring teeth
      garments
          hair
      nails & body.
            fixing stained glass
      into a floor.
            making beds
      & arranging carpets
            & cushions.
      playing musical glasses
            filled with water.
      picture making
            stringing garlands
      & preparing perfumes.
            magic or sorcery.
      cooking & sewing.
            verse-making games.
      the art of acquiring
          property
      by means of incantations

      & shaving white wood
            smooth in the shadows

a book
      is a
number of
      sheets of
paper
      bound or
stitched
      together
a list of
      horses
entered
      in a race
a pack of
      gold-leaf
six tricks
      taken by one
side
      a bundle of
tobacco leaves
      cut in ½
longitudinally
      & without
      the
      stems
      unoriginal
      according
      to rule
      literal.

SONNET

at the Rhapsody & Squash a tankard yes & a
dog at the door: *fuck!*   *fuck-fuck!*
fuck-fuck-fuck!   at The Flowering Blast

a nip   at The Gap In Your Understanding
a sore toe & a quick mind   or that must
have been in The Mottled Earwig   who will

agree with what next? continuing on in
in a (strangely revolving) silence   so send
help. to The Piebald Piglet. at The Legless

Egg a glass of diminuendo mountain cascade
    in such materials our difficulty under a
cone of light scratching a history: swollen

knuckles of an old man's hand. this one did
that then & then that one did this. & then
& then. love, life, happiness-&-grabbing & a

grippingly bitter tender thought on *fuck-fuck!*
tenders lost. behind a shop at The Dank Stump
    recording from across the street in The

Turning Worm   in detail   in impotence under
        the table where I tell you
                this.

sirens   brakes   impact at full speed
the police keep busy bless them   that's a roof
over my head not a leprachaun's inkcap

or part thereof deft steps & confident
up there atilt on broken slates to
keep rain out & the clouds in place

Sonata 439

posted a parcel to Berlin   dreaming   that
book arrived intact too out of the blue
by the way   cheers   I must type this up

in italics side-down because the other
daisywheel's dandelion forsythia broom
yellow for beginning green follows through

they say but let's not swallow too many old idylls
like   well   they should look to their
health   you know me Mary   having the gods

   in you isn't all that

    odd

    o o o

The first raindrop in the dust sculpts a
cup-shaped hole, many such bunched merge
to become tiny streamlets, in turn making
little channels, loosening & carrying away
earth-particles, until the run-off is con-
centrated first into irregularities, then
rills, then gullies, then streams … Minúte
crustaceans hatch from eggs that may have
been blowing in the drought for half a century
or more & over hundreds of miles from where
they were laid by their long-dead parents
in the desert. Item: crisp levels. Speleology:
the study of holes in the ground.

Coming home late tired after work through the
medieval centre of an Italian town, nobody about,
winter, fog following through the streets,
splashed lines ribbed & whorled, rhythms gapped,
fluent dash thrill dash shrink into lyrical
young-plant-time in shadows under the trees.
Those were the days. These. Footsteps echoed.
Everything closed. I stopped outside a bookshop
on a corner. In the centre of its window
tastefully arranged – a circle set in a square –
on a plinth bedded in silk, the work in translation
of a writer of my own country, in resplendence –
busy old fool, unruly sun – lay. Oh no genius
of course, shine on the wings – whatever *that*
is – but a reputation & a blur of portable quotations.
And green, green, a saleable country, the very
colour of money.

>   countless little threads
>   (this is known as the run-off)
>   thin film on smooth slopes
>   (this is known as sheet flow)

Now the coffin is upright in front of the tomb. Now
a priest performs the ritual of the Opening of the

Sonata

Mouth ... Royal Scribe & Steward, Overseer of Royal
Cattle, Scribe of Divine Offerings, his black heart
is placed on scales & balanced against the white
feather of truth while Am-mut, Devourer, a sort
of ravenous dog-god, waits hungrily for the result.
Then as now, count on it, wealth & status will
see you through.

  that small liquid
    sound is
  that wine I'd
    forgotten about
  still fermenting
    in its demi-john
  systole
    filled in Leitrim
  in a little cottage
    on a side of a hill
  diastole
    & forgotten
  years ago
    while
      we
        travelled
          across
    difficult surfaces
  overground/underground
dreaming/waking life/death
    dark/light out/in
      hey!
  & years
(to take time as a map –
  fluent –
dissolving as you live –
  how then did
feathers evolve –
  anyway?)
is it
  the fly's
energetic
  zigzag
the way the
  buzz shifts
a tone
  just before
landing
  is it

    systole/diastole
        I wonder
… potable?
        [& landing the
    other side
        of the web –
hah!]
        hardly.

oh look these artists
have also portrayed
themselves standing
among their cattle

sitting beside huts
hunting with bows &
arrows in their hands
dancing with masks

on their heads. it's
the outer shell of a
grass-seed not a fly's
wing a male & female

tension in the weather.
as. if. is that a sound
it makes on impact?

•

passing a bookshop
on a corner in fog
one night in November
late after work tired

a new prize-writer
bedded in silk caught
my/even here in this
border settlement on

the banks of the
Styx pushed hard
by the industry –
hard – threading

us all into the
under-padding in
the doormat to
the temple of/

oh so tired after
work crossing a
piazza in fog &
about to be en-

lightened [   ]
caught my tired
eyes but then
I woke up (this

must be) strange faces
reflected upside-
down in the liquid
in my cup/when a

door slams shut
& I was stirring
my coffee idly
thinking of

that night years ago –
this strange concertedness
of getting – *isolated* –
yes – if that's it –

flicked aside &
suddenly pale green
palpi extend a
predatory greeting

for peace & commodious
living with names
in the black notebooks
of those bright

careers that darken
your difficult path/
my dear I/*hah!*

•

to remember memory
a map as you make
it breathing breath-
ing the co-

ordinates
        corridors
rats in a tube
hi cherryjam please

yes not a word into
the fabric favours
privileges safeties
mesh & fix/not/step-

ping lightly over
the cobbles/not a
word/of the piazza
through the fog

hovering past
closed up streets
tight & lit home
now to my wife

step by filtering
so-called inanimate
objects step tapping
the lattice where

flowers & stones flow
through their doubles
to meet you or slip
through their crystals

to *be* you twisting
at their cross-points
in silence flushing
through diamond-haze

following a sun
following them: I am
ready (& confused)
stopped over paper

fingers nimble singing
dumb: here is the weather
here is the news. by the
mantis playing.

   home now to my
wife now my child my
 papers in silence in
    a box godwot.

II

    Grasp sparrow's tail

                single whip

play guitar

                lean forward

white crane spreads its wings

                brush knee & twist – step –

play guitar

                brush knee & fix – step –

step forward

            deflect

                downward

                    intercept

& punch

                draw back (split) & push

SONNET

Here we are in a Photograph: arrived: the Palace of Art
Administration. Mouth-flash. Hum. Bow. Loners need not
apply to this hill station, I've been there (I think)
in this story this afternoon and know. Turn page.
Help Wanted. She looked (to make a mistake you need
Rules in the first place) not back, but at the outside,
not inside, squat slabs upside-down on the desk, sun
hitting little prisons of dark over time sliding away.

Fine. Remember you know nothing. To give noticing ghosts
back going past glass here again sideways a second (split)
into you. Remember. Angle-glancing, maybe-catching, that
irregular verb *must-do*. Nothing. And that nothing changes.
Remember that. To slip your shadow past the lake. Rememb-
ering that to slip your shadow past the lake. There. *Kak!*
goes a gull, *I quite agree! Quite quite quite quite qui...*
Gold, Golf, Golgotha, Golly, Gondola, Gong, Good.
Heart's Gold, Golf.

I hold them to the light. I hold you to your word. You do.
It is. The past comes through. I don't know. What *are* they
building? That's a foghorn. That's a hammertap. Taptap. Life
as a file of photo opportunities. Brightness falls from
the lair. Freeze. Smile. Look Casual. Sidelong. Hand to chin.
To cheek. Turn. Stop. Surprise. "All swans are white."

ARC

snow crystals
on the skylight

snow drifting
& falling

from black treetops
in a bright dust

snow silencing the street
& exciting the kids

when December my
father in December

falling to pass through
mystery, tired,

died. sunlit.
whiteness. whiteness

under starlight
whiteness underfoot

on the street
on the bridge

to the beach
in December moonlight

bluewhite greywhite
piling on wires

& on the tops of cars
windowledges doorsteps

falling & gathering
my father.

who could
would

& did

swim cutting a smooth arrow outwards

to that island
& back & around
again &

won

is gone

leaving a trace.
moving through

the crystalline
world of a grain

of salt sodium
chloride sodium

chloride rank upon
rank of atoms in their

pattern, poised.
my face, his quietness.

SECTION

there it is.
this is a very
strong x-ray
source. shut

the door in
the wall & go.
face east. bow.
it is over.

tiny
flecks. flicks
of consciousness.
we named them

& we named them
good. wrong.
good. follow
yr keyboard

down to a last
attaching taut
scrap of *súgán*
caught between

forward slash
& @. haven't
you learnt any
thing at all?

that a circle through
two given points may
have its centre anywhere
on the right bisector
of their joining line

& that a circle touching
two given intersecting
straight lines has its
centre anywhere on either
of the lines bisecting
the angles between them

A SONG
(& A DANCE)

Remember that clematis
plant Ric brought us here to
Dublin dug in by the new
place in flower now on
a wall in spring
mindful of how it goes
in quiet radiance as all
does worth the caring for –
tag to Ric's tact and
a reminder.

•

Remember that clematis
limber through lattice
in flat ice flowers
on a wall
being spring in
this climate growing
in radiance beyond all noise
as everything does
worth caring for –
tag to Ric's hand
and a reminder. Grace.

•

Remember that clematis
climbing in silence
twisting limbs through
tacked lattice embered
everywhere in flat
shockflowers on a wall
being spring in this.
Yes. Stays.

•

Trembling clematis
(its crowded flowers, its
teeming greens) in a light
breeze now set out that
year Ric came to visit us
by the south-facing wall
mindful of how it shows
in quiet radiance
bits of evidence too
complex to hold still and
still not see through that
end-beginning nonsense to
the no-frame of life beyond
our lives – tag to Ric's plant.

A reminder. And a dance.

•••

left out bin
clapped hands
dog slips in

closed windows
plugged kettle
in touched a tree

nod again decide
again negotiate
the gate

the railings
& all that inhale
exhale bus goes

by cleared up
table then around
a pebble drops in

time have you noticed
ice glass kids at
school around

then about bus
down street cross
the floor the mat

slipped off shoes
            dance

angle of the house
mirror doorway stair-
well hey! around &

then/clap hands
tap the tap the sink
step architrave

my notes yr song
quotes fall from
the air all dance

take this from that
put those there
return to begin

again gain grace by
degrees only watch
yr step there &

practise here | you
are holding yr breath
here the air gives

back its light to
spare here fear
is falling into the

   past all dance glint
   dancing away

  where
    is
  that
    tree
  bent
    severe-
  ly
    to
  the
    left
  I
    remember
  (it)
    below
  me
    as
  I
    write
  a
    not
  a
    power
  a
    birch
  black-
    ened
  by
    traffic
  gives
    small
  green
    leaves
  this
    slice
  of
    bright-
  ness

        in
the
    just-
begun
      over
the
    black
rail-
      ings
in
    the
garden?

cars.

a
    dog
bark-
    ing.

sirens.

a
    bus
stops

  all danced

  all dance away

•••

Around a loose thread and

      remember that clematis
      plant Ric brought us here to
      Dublin dug in by the new
      place in flower now on
      a wall in spring –

have a cup of tea I said.
have a cup of tea. I think
I will. I did. (the circle's
an intriguing totem.) stir it.
and start again.

ah-ha! *they said peering*
down at the specimen in a
circle round the table

stone circles   literary circles
circles under the eyes

       – twisting through its
        lattice emblems everywhere
        trembling teeming in a
        light breeze mindful of
        how it goes when it goes
        to bits our lives mistakes
        radiance – a limberwort –
        it is – yes, this – and
        failing tags or evidence –
        mind my moustache – what's
        new? – little understood.
        so very little understood.

        remembering that clematis
        plant Ric brought us here…

---

i.m.: Ric Caddel

○   ○   ○

SONNET

I was telling you
I suppose. Step by
step. It was filtering
down. (Also page 23.
As it now stands.)
He ingests the curse.
It is eating him.
Mock-scream. Children's
scenarios among sirens
through alleyways. I'm
God. How do you do.
How do you do. Let's
look over this balcony.
What's that? Brightness
falls from the air.
Events in old-time
poetry as they were
fan dazzle at the
smoot £2 @ hour
(flat rate) & watching
(close your eyes)
in this place until
some cats engage in
the Drama of Life
under a digger
swallowing worries
emphatic packages of
time everything around
the while in its
place to its own
end a friend ("Site
normal. Nothing to
report.") where
through silence
now that I remember
it lies take shape
quite sculptural too

sugar standing in
a garden paper &
pen & contacts like
that persistent fly & the
telephone & such bits
of other miscellanea
stick like

white crane spreads its wings

                                          brush knee & twist

    stick like that

grasp sparrow's tail
   single whip
play guitar
   lean forward
white crane spreads its wings
   brush knee & twist
step
   play guitar
brush knee & fix – step –
   step forward
deflect downward
   intercept &
punch
   draw back (split) & push

cross hands

cross hands folding

III

SONG

On the field of beginning
a ripple hits a ripple
where a cat barks
and a dog denies it
over the other side
of a wall over there

but here you sit and listen
where Do Not Grab
is tacked to your shed
and leaves move in a light
breeze in a sideways light.
Spider: beware.

The angle of repose
and the angle of agitation
fuse together at base
to build a place from
nothing and go on.
Do not grab.

It's Istin isn't it –
for a high level of confidence
& oedema, headache, flushing,
dizziness, nausea, fatigue,
palpitations, somnolence,
abdominal pain, altered

bowel habits, arthralgia,
asthemia, dyspepsia, dyspnoea,
gingival hyperplasia,
gynaecomastia, impotence,
increased urinary frequency,
mood changes, muscle cramps,

myalgia, pruritis, rash,
visual disturbances,
erythema multiforme,
jaundice & hepatic enzyme
elevations…
in the field of beginning

to draw a line in the snow
melting into each side
of the argument
on the side of a mountain
before arriving where
you'd not intended to go:

a bit of lyric goes a long long way
so on our way back from
that place a glow – & a sting.

Now, Devonex for children too.
'You'll like the way they like it.'
Local irritative papular eruptions.

Leaves – needles – cones –
after a storm the storm's work
& birds sing.

It's Istin, isn't it?

Honey, I'm home.

O O O

SONNET

ripple-zeros on a roadside pool. crescent of shell in the sand.
they have to keep naming these places.
if.

      yes yes (cloud the mirror) then inside the
      world's space
      hang on   this hat's too tight.

          pinecone in dogshit on path.

              to make a table
              you need a gun
              filled with rhetoric.

                    so you're another – what?
                    storyteller twiddling dice
                    in a game called Risk? two parts

                          confection, one part grit.

SONNET

      this three-&-a-half inch long

                reddish brown/black

worm

          lives year-round in

                    Alaskan & Pacific Northwest

  glaciers

      the Ice Worm

& probably eats

    spores
          bacteria
               algae
                    pollen

  but

            no one

is

    absolutely sure.

to make a table
you need power

pierced by childhood.
then move on.

       •

        so you're another lyricist?
        my mother
            remembers
        yr brother.

SONNET

when I follow patterns of scratches on the
surface of my desk they lead me to my little
pop-up book of knowledge in which moons – in profile,
& laughing – & ringed planets in gold dye on a gauze
curtain [verb illegible] behind which my wristwatch
pips. here we are. I tell my little ones it's the
fairies calling. we speak into my watch. once upon
a time there was a duck…

        shadow of

    yes   crow   I   across street

think   gone

            by   on

opposite rooftop

    black on black

    a breeze in the ivy clicks.

SONNET

then I woke up.

paring a pencil
carefully, its
frill, its dark

dust, a fly's
shadow rubbing
its forelegs
together

by a
window

green
blue
red

(thank you for that)

bees
shad
pine-trees

rats in the tube
hi! cherryjam please

yes not a word into
the fabric favours
privileges safeties
mesh & fix/not step-

ping lightly over
the cobbles/of the
piazza through
the fog –

& clipped my nails
with pleasure &
gathered thinking
their sharp-pointed

curves cut with
pleasure thinking
together into a
little heap

(

						)

momentary picture
of birds in flight
over ocean & tipped
them into the

wastepaper basket
beside me with a
small filigree
of ticking sound –

home now to my papers
in silence in a box
godwot _____

_____

foam

                      ice

bale

      castor

blunt as that –
   to live
watching
   never expecting to
participate

or directly anyway
   dimple a surface
tilt an
   event to yr will
set a date

on a page
   start
startled
   shifting sideways
again where

all these little
   pieces fall

SONNET

asymmetry
      in the feathers
too shows as a
      thickened axis
which lies
      closer to the leading
than to the
      trailing
          edge.

as a result
      each feather
acts like a
      tiny wing
directing air more
      quickly over its upper surface
& providing
      extra
lift
      lift
to each wing
      as a whole.

            kick-flip
            ½-pipe
            tail-slide
                grind
                ollie
                cannonball
            pop-shove-it
            kick-flip-to-indy
            hand-plant
            drop-in
            caveman
                bale.

•

to make a table
           you need theory-in-excelsis
pierced by groundswell.

         •

        so you're another
                novelist?
        tell me yr novelty.

○ ○ ○

---

if a food source
is close the dance
is a circular pattern;
if a food source

is distant the dancing
indicates its direction
with respect to the sun
by the angle of the

straight run to the
vertical

so:

here is the news &
    weather.

peeling a little bark
to get the smell of the tree feeding.

breathing for a
time (sign here)
watermarks
among sticky

reticula a flower
quirked & green
& stencilled with
a paler green irr

egularly across
& round the edge.
I'll write with a
pen thanks did or

move among

sense-accommodating
loops (twisting)
(garbled in the mach
ine) bumped against

black over the river
on a low bridge
along the old track
past shop garage

house pub church
past a quietness
where a tree had
been past the shallow

river down below
f(ol)lowing the trail
disconsolate past it
all step to then on

the way to my/or/in
here is (   )
weather

into a brick
wall.

whether little bits
of money stick out
of passing cloud
paper money shaking

catching light now &
then then losing it
lost altogether or
not. lovely moments.

o lots of lovely moments.
kin. where distinctly
rich meet distinctly
poor & drop down law

whispering gold-gold
through a polar smile
or two in the middle
ground. I don't know.

what? a kitten nibbles a twig.
& when breezes
shake

leaves a little it pretends
amazement. mica-
glint-

s. corm. here (   ) is the
(   ) news.
paint

the gate. fix the hinges. prepare
the wood & the
path.

paint the wall beside it.
white. let that be
that.

black.
a dot. a
dark dot
moving

hang on
a sec a
spider
quiet in

a corner
sound of a
bee at its
abc

scraping a
nectary rain
on glass to
the side of

yr face as it
sizzles is
it & back to-
wards each tiny

towards each
tiny percussion
the word for
"word" write

down look
up excise
you play I
play tin op

ener in yr
hand of an
evening
cook talk

sketch need
ing to rel
ax dancing
needing I

suppose I
is that a
question?

is that
Goodie-Two-
Shoes at
the door.

jaggeds.
oh sure.
a cushy
number

for the
peccable
each mouth
moving

someone
else's
greed-
focus

snapping
neatly into
each clear
prediction.

I saw the
word *variegated*
follow a
curved

line subtle
over a
pebble's
smooth

to its cut
reservoir
at the side
there

asper. the
word *time*
the word
pity.

that's the
end of that
argument –
a bubble

of plusses
floats pops
in the half-
dark with

a spirited
chirrup of
a sparrow in
the rain.

grey
grey-black
blue-black
black

grey-black
white.

right.
you call
that sweet?

working
day & night
for a pitt
ance for

pen & ink
& such ex
otica the
rent 2

sticks click
on a winter
appletree
odd bird

   tip

this is my
favourite
time I think.
task: press

yr upper
& lower
lips to-

gether
ever so

gently

like this:
chill breeze.
listen.

what melts so
well into an
other & an-
other with

a
deft
flick

& a straight
face *h'mm*
well what can
I teach?

deep blue
to black
then grey

folding
to centre
pouring

burning
bursting
dark stain

diminishing
to its small
upstreaked

curled to
the left
where it
thickens

white grey
fringe on
dark grey
  is it on
    red

yr good
neighbours
the Photo-
Copies

Wainscot
  Trellis
    & Fury

right smack
bang in the
middle of yr
Rorschach blot!

•

a
  bus
stops.

idles
  &
moves
  on

its
  plane
in
  section

dividing

down
  along
a
  street
brief
  glisten
of

```
    ink
as
   yr
thinking
   for
a
   time
here
   now
dries
   behind
each
   next
step
   one
little
   conman
two –

two
   very
happy
   anti-
clock-
   wise
ideas
   that
do a
   quick
flash &
   tangle
together
   then
make
   up.
yes?


         •
```

yap said
the dog
yap-yap.
hack

through that
& start again.
too true.
where's my

map? to
make a table
you need a
leg to

stand on.
so you're
another
pragmatist?

pass me that
hammer!

hang up
jacket sit
down by
the window

where books
papers search
pen rent in
its envelope

in a pot I
can hear what
must be music
on tape

blasted out
but far enough
out of the way
to be a

whisper-pattern
over traffic
paddling along
a corridor

dip-dap
to yr name
on a plate
on a door

      Boast of women
      Boast of beauty
      Blanching of faces
      Most difficult at night
      Marrow of charcoal
      Third part of a wheel
      Sweetest tree

& there
meet print –
    Christ
it's cold! –

each detail
rippled at
each point

so that
nothing seems
to fit

till you hit
gravel & yr
keel keeps.

CODA

In Tzuba the expression of movement downward as expressed by the stationary observer on the ground is *tlel* meaning "less up" and movement upwards *utze*, meaning "less down". When movement stops the object is said to be either up (*atè*) or down (*ut*) but these carry the suffix *cling* to express what is thought of as a circular journey (however small) completed. So *atècling* expresses an upward journey completed as *utcling* a journey downward. So: *Utcling na tzaba na nabnana stlo*, "A bird has landed on the ground."

•

I don't know. Not an act of mere will. Not sheer assertion. Downward river corrasion, mirror-decisions in limelight, selected adventures, interviews, photos, things that go pop in the ego, I put my cup down (you've been around, I see) and gaze steadily towards if not quite directly into the centre of this reconditioned limbo. Game, set. Shake hands. The forms of escape are ridiculous: I will face you and fight (said the corpse). *I've* got a Loss-of-Confidence. What have *you* got? I've got/ but. *Myth, ignorance, misinformation & wishful thinking* whisper the wings of the dragonfly. I've got notes, you've got the music. (I've got an interview, you've got the job.) Chorus. *Là-bas*. In what key? Who's Willy Nilly? Some background murmur (is not the chorus). What have *you* got? A postcard. Of course you want to be happy. Of course you want peace. Of course you want to strike out on a new path: of course. Our diaphanous, pliant bubble extending, contracting easily, pat, re-asserting its set limits. Tap. That knocking he said – taptap – can you hear it? A Moroccan Woodpecker. Oh yes, I *see* it.

•

The first raindrop in the dust sculpts a cup-shaped hole, many such bunched merge to become tiny streamlets, in turn making little channels, loosening & carrying away earth-particles, until the run-off is concentrated first into irregularities, then rills, then gullies, then streams ... Minúte crustaceans hatch from eggs that may have been blowing in drought for half a century or more & over hundreds of miles from where they were laid by their long-dead parents in the desert. Item: pressed layers. Speleology: the study of objects beyond reach – space, air ... *that* should do it – the study of circular objects beyond our reach ...

SONNET

did you
    get that
money I
    sent good
for
    headache
heartache
    amor vincit
omnia that
    or
sun-dazzle
    & a quick
shoal of
    bright fish
developing
    sideways
under a
    keel or
crux of
    a window-
frame in
    the snow
a magpie
    banks &
lands
    must that
that must
    be

    the need for
    flattened bark-
    dwelling insects
    to get away from
    predators on
    treetrunks may
    well have
    provided the

       selective pressure
       that led to the
       evolution of
       wings

must
    that
must be
    the password.

then I woke up.

       •

"up in the trees
what do you
need?"
    fingers & eyes &
    a fine
    spine.

down on the ground
what do you
feel?
    slips very quickly
    curriculum
    vitae.

rosehip picked to make
a tonic for the kids
in winter

bits of sky given back
upside-down &
rippled

    a wind that turns a
    leaf on the
    ground

down &
around &
back.

then I woke up.

•

black.

to open
(this is
an apple)
my notebooks

to close
them again
sudden
escaped
song

typewriter
blunt on
its desk
in front

of me em

phatically
plastic steel
rubber maybe
a copper fil

ament or two
becoming ob
solete at speed
yes is not

cannot
be my Brother.

sand

song

Dáil

Dalí

god the linguist
making the sign
of Examination

   this street
   has a tree
     in it

/tilt///spin/
six tips of a single
snowflake's crystals
in the wind

black silver sparkles
in the sun I
turn to (check)
it's

gone surprise &
delight open &
write it the light
down.

SONNET

From your previous life you have brought
to this life 502 catties of sesame oil
& 100 copper coins. You are straightforward
& talented. You will be able to acquire
a lot of money from many sources but will
have a minor accident.
         Dig down: root haze. Look up: blue
         fibre. It's wonderful to hear leaves
         on trees again though. To get into
         bed beside you as excited as this.
         Years of grinding technique roll back
         to be imploded through one or two pages
         of pure fire. Never thought...
The clutter of yr shed is different
from yr English language, no? Yes.
Down on that track I definitely tried
to get a glimpse of what I thought
effable: crossing the dateline into
a clock. Rip.
         Child whimpering, adept, tangible flanges
         of a language that held him in: you'll
         tell me, I said. Who did. You did. Nipped
         in the bud. They said they might. Right.
         Are nipples oak galls?
Writing, deleting, writing again, patient, persistent,
dogged to the point of/(?)/is what was reflected on
that surface leering up, magnetic & stupid, up from
whose hopelessness you could eat through to the next
depth barely.
         Site normal. As to the proportions of the cell:
         yr trivia is as engaging as my trivia. And sticks.
         Then palps to the paralysed hymenoptera. Busy
         busy busy...
You will suffer from diarrhoea for a while
then die on a sunny day, but it will rain
on the day of yr funeral. Your coffin will
be made in a hurry because the Lonely Star

will be approaching you. Although you will
have two sons & one daughter to carry yr
coffin to the cemetery, it will not be a
splendid funeral.
    Daddy, Daddy...

        Your corpse will be
            Your funeral will take place
        You will die between
            the ages of
        You will have two sons and
            one daughter to
        and your funeral will be a
            splendid affair
Daddy, Daddy (curious shimmer of word-haze
over a wall) *can I show you magic?*
        And back to ceramics. Repeating meetings
        in a windowless coop where committees
        web & clog, minutes pouring – pouring
        without end – down a rusty old
You will go to a relative's party
catch a disease and then die
        down a rusty old chute diagonal to
        & entering the side of a building
        whose irregular flecks of black &
        white are once thought to have read
        Poison or *Position* or *Person* or
        Pension – smoothly uncoiling from the
        tube – glutinous firework English
        from China – or *Para-* something...
        dise? surely not –
It will/You will/It will/on the day of
your/two old monks/carry/funeral/splendid

Tig

STEPPING

I

[BLESSING THE ANIMALS]

then
    the spring-born population stays put
in its region of birth
    the Great Lakes of North America.

then
    of the autumn-born population
⅓ hibernates
    while the remaining ⅔
set out southwards
    on a narrow unwavering route.
it's a journey of 3000 kilometres
    down to south Texas/northern Mexico.

on arrival they gather in one or two
    valleys on particular conifers
in their millions
    & rest there till spring
& mate.

then this immense blizzard of wings
    begins to move northwards
travelling in a more leisurely way
    feeding & laying their eggs along the route…

        the train's shadow
        flickering over the fields

the Monarch is a long-lived butterfly
    each individual surviving approximately
one year.
    their migration pattern is as follows

        a child nearby
        at a window

        (migration pattern is as)

where the world
tracks past a

very young child
so happy so

taken aback
she

sings. (follows) & it beats
disclosing enclosing

flash! fold *flash!*
close slit show shock

blind shock black
shock/light exuding

over the visible
light intruding

on the visible
light corroding

the leaves leaving
only the light.

their

dispersal   patterns

are as   follows.

map.   stop.

count.   then

immense   upsurge

white   red

amber   dark

the need for flattened bark-dwelling insects
to get away from predators on tree-trunks may
well have provided the selective pressure that
led to the evolution of wings – between rains
we lay listening lay waiting – you know me…

    rain on glass to the side of yr face

        a door shut in a corridor

II

[BACKYARD]

so that.

      when
            leaves
                  stiffen
                        flare
disconnect

& quietly
        fall detached from
their place at

each point (exact) landing in even
circles anding at different
times the

      different

on flat green grass & (echo – tussled hair –
handshake) litter   collect
that

different (or) touching a windowpane where
drops gather ( ) difference ( ) &
or different

( ) colours even. stopped outside a fruitshop
on a corner
warmer

than December remember hands
pink that weigh/&/
gilt scales

splinters of pieces of vivid
boxes shelves
fruitsmell

Tig 521

in passing talking to I was
talking to
you were

saying quick/shadow-flash
(pigeons) quick
past

sunlit walls then (pattern)
then gone/look.
what?

stunned/back from hospital
on the way back too
back to the wall

my old dead
father in
shadow

in the Shadow of
hearing for
sure

its articul
ate whis
per |

core to granulated
crust my
dull

moves & days/
thunder-
clashes

& a train overhead.
it is porous
&

dangerous it is
porous/it is
pour it.

[WATERWAY]

    suddenly
yr tomb a little
block of stone
placed fast to
   the spot

  yr name
       gone
  not
       suddenly
  sudden
       ly
  yes
       gone
  gone
       traces
  to be
       sure but
  gone
       vanished
  into
       air
  take it
       to where
  you will
       but
  cut
       where's
  my
       map?
  where's
       my
  hammer
       gone?
  who
       said
  goodbye

```
            &/from
one side
        here
not wide
        fly
true
        to
the other
        but
    deaf
    frail
    blind
step & then
        a step
            (gone)
reading out
        reading out
the signs
        for you
in the park
        loud
step
        & then a
step
        ash
flame
        holly
yellow
        & bloated
in the
        end
the
        drugs
(step)
        given you
oh to
        help you
to help
        you yes
```

```
        the packet
                says
        Lethe
                or
        Lever
                or
        Leave It
                can you
        hear it?
                from one
        little
                drug
        company
                to
        another
                with
        love
                a sort
        of circ-
                ulating
        siren-
                echo
        quietly
                stitched
        in
                to
        that
                logo
        that
                gets
        round
                to
        help
                you
        (ste/p)
                yes
        leave
                now
        but
```

                suddenly
    to
                grieve
    what's
                that?
    let's
                argue
    (gone)
                where's
    my biro?
                my note-
    pad?
                what date's
    today?
                is it
    raining?
                my news-
    paper?
                shoes?
    dog?
                tell me
    tell me

       colour pictures
                moving snaps
    slipping channels
                shadows
                &
       quietness
                &
                fathers
            whirl
                about
         a name
         is probably a
         definite article
         in somebody's
         statute in sub-
         terranean heaven

somewhere but
here
    a blank.

    step &
        then a
    step.

[BACKYARD]

v-ripples echoing
action underwater
sing amor for shelter
forever from sharks

in that dark welter
of trouble-dogging-
the-innocent in this
Holding Centre for

Continuing Re-education
curiously thought to
consist – down to the
root Lie of the Land –

Life. gulls sparrows
bees feeding a heron
a cat spider in wait
brittle reflections

on still pools oakleaf
folded in a muddy crevice
my left hand to my right
quick blur my fingers

my way of life. how does
god remember all the
things in the right place
of us? how does he stick

them on? are we just
photographs talking (I
put the daisywheel
in its box) or what? my

daughter (4). name
on a plate on a door.
tree-sure treasure
a small spider quiet

in a corner covering
for a time what appears
there moving – glory! –
& spectacular sensations

developing under the
tongue. well now turn-
ing over the papyrus
here it strikes us

one life one elong-
ated crisis (with
modulations) icy
fingers of discomfort

in the lower back each
stiff hair to its nerve-
cell (notify yr solicitor
when that picket of *ifs*

cuts across yr precious
precarious spinney) alert
& ready: "comfort" is

    wrong. yes?

        &
        a song
        shh
        is
        I was told

        stack
        blade
        bit

                    is
                    work

                    work?

shaving the white wood smooth in the shadows

quite   thank you for that

a wave
            collapsing on its patch of sand

                        a
                            fresh
                        a
                            is

not so very long ago
                            quietly one Saturday
morning
            detached

            one piece of old hat
            deserves another
            after all

                        whittle
                        gouge
                        stop

                        work
                        they said

                        a song
                        they said
                        note
                                don't
                        do you?
                        a

sh
ap
e.
ah.

out of the
chequerwork
barbed dazzle
of Difficulty-

in-Life suddenly
I espied me a
gap in the defences
& Light's

eager
molecular chain
in frenzy just
without. an ABC

turn it
over look in
peer down dizzy
to find (*then*

crossing the
mountains we
got stranded
one night) –

high gloss low
visibility – in
the undancing face
of a boulder in yr

       path:

Calculated Greed.

fat stem.
tiny branches.
enormous yellow flowers.

too short too partisan too frag
mented too unintelligible the
issue too difficult to decypher
who's who in this & what is it any-

way an accelerating bubble on a swollen
tide – machines of war memory perception –
whose meanings can't any more be pre-
figured or absorbed cultures inverted

to prey on not "cradle" "civilizations"
lulling or eliminating peoples for the
use of a few invisible manipulators of
no country or allegiance – theft –

parasitic on a scale never before thought
possible to succeed – eating up humanity.
eating it up. meanwhile old-world lyrics
get prizes in small quaint corners. &

good luck to them. *An Ceangal:* in this
particular out-building to the Forgotten
Gaelic Tradition I find that Blackbird of
Anywhere-At-All quite likely to be in two

minds on one branch. leaf-swish. between
your dictionary & its air-shapes, an inter-
mission. try harder. bigger vistas, less
credulity. *cementery* is good. yes?

sing Amor.

III

[A FALLING LEAF]

cryptic snippets in yr pockets
by some loose change on the floor
lie quiet as you lie with her
yr day's dazed thoughts on buses
libraries the street.

it's supposed to add up to something
& be greater than the sum of its parts
too not statistics through the window you're
always gazing graphs & diagrams of the heart
without scale or co-ordinates
unlike the "simplicities of nature"
or many aspects of a discipline
presuming to think you know
the mind ready & the scene set.

.

people have to expect to be seen
to expect to be believed
innocent of bureaucracy
insistent the tune
slips through level or not.

people can be born to expect to be loved
not conned insist to be
the source out of which
a music issues level irregular
November   October   anywhere.

things written between
things selected things new
& collected things &   so on.
a business of. & filing.
can conned people expect understanding?

.

orbiting around that great liquid spine of the river

                                        older

salmon & sea trout in & out of the worlds of
salt & fresh water

older

rarest plant   purple milk vetch   low-growing perennial
whimbrel & tufted frunnock
fruit an elongated hairy pod

                        older

I took my children to the sea
            a dog barked

    they build sandcastles
I built castles we had
3 then 9
    castles
poisoning
    watched planes arrive

suddenly

older

[PICKING PERSIMMON]

distinctly through
the night air trains

through otherwise
silence – contact –

toy-like parallel
movements where machinery

clocks into place.
listen I saw what

I meant you saw
& the sunny external

world slid past over
yr shaded spectacles

& for the sake of
the rhythm I suppose

of the train on its
track you smiled.

it all takes you back.

under an intimate
intense cone of light

on a page on a desk
among books in the night

to return upturn upset
visit obsessive hating

obsessed teaching the
cocky ignorant well-to-do

offspring of the European
upper echelons to

limp along in something
like an intelligible

legible *béarlagair*
tax free on the button…

I always liked being there
that dark & haunting house

off the South Circular
at the canal end where

colossal mirrors
spread out their

cloth ducks in flight
across a wall

*oranges & lemons
& the bells*

of St Clement's &
the strangeness

of flickering eyes
that are blind –

oh movements
continuous &

formal forgive
us our futures!

& loneliness.
& affection

that atom
incandescent

in the tune
the train's

shadow flickering
over the fields

mountains passing
(a city, distant)

gull-spots wheeling

a child nearby
at a window

where the world
tracks past a

very young child
so happy so

taken aback
she sings…

                         & farre

                                        exelle

                        all other strowing

                                                     herbes

             for to decke up houses

                                                                  slate

     web

                  clay

                             weed

pebbles

             withered root

                                             dust

                                                        litter

       spider

                flicker of leaves lodged at the stub

       a tree

is a multiparticular planar miracle

is a book   an electronic blur   a minúte variation hook

is a door   a still   my notes   hats   quotes

the shadows moving in the breeze in the sunlight
beside the white house outside the village by the sea

change

———

found a nest
in a hedge

its centre a
weave of hair
from the family's
dog

silky oval precise
ly birdbody-size
no egg   some plastic
string.

———

CODA

[A PLACE TO STAY]

Go little thing   be good
black thread   spicule   white
solid radiant basis
carved cradled care-driven materials
twisting textures
to him who has his senses still
baaah! goes the train on the line
yes & twisting she moves
& still – to balance –
arthritic & pert places in the spine
that plain stab-of-the-beak
& twist – *baaah!* – chance – a hand –
step – spread in the light –
see shade you don't dread
thread where you are a long
time-thing radiant
bright cone – *baaah!* – too –
not a word –
dough lolly loot
dough lolly loot.
good.

•

Profile to phonepiece
edged by light
a tenseness in the silence of the room
in the time it takes
catching a tangle of cables
the sun beyond the window
takes   it takes to &
the time it takes to
find out   is it
is it
really alright?

•

Nets in flight in the half-light
& has his senses still
& sense & has stillness
& sense
start up the stairs again
as early as you can

    there can be no very
to carry yr cares
    there can be no very
to pen the tune
    there can be no very
black melancholy
to him who
hurry
let's hurry across to the island
to see the notetaker
         soulmaker
           soulmate…

woke   here is the
nine o'clock   in the
temperate zones   when
I   you said to me

I see (nine) reading
my   quiet have I not
been (news) thinking
of you were there are

    some gaps here.

Assembly of hounds

Otherworldly sustenance

Shelter of the wounded

Power of the weak

Dregs of clothing

Most noble goodliness

SONNET

quietly   more quietly go
playfully   accept
except

───────────────

quietly
      more quietly still
smiling

───────────────

she left a leaf on my desk

───────────────

it fell

───────────────

tree-bit

───────────────

down. (earth)
        that.
land on it.
    ignition

───────────────

the word for *quick*
in this language

a dog at a door
barricade

───────────────

blackback tilts & turns
robin under privet

───────────────

what a zero glass cube
to write up

───────────────

plant a little seed
in the big black earth

───────────────

wait

───────────────

a fly stopped on a stone
grooming

───────────────

hare   *giddy person*

                           otter   *water snake*

retaliate   *demons*

                            tor   *belly*

vanquish   *and*

                           weel   *use*

whisper   *synonymous*

                           zone   *colour*

zymurgy   *maker of leaven*

───────────────

she left a leaf on my desk

CODA CODA

SONNET ODE: BLESSING THE ANIMALS

ONE

    that tendency
    & I see towards
    bisymmetry

                              until she was 49 & then
                              only because she found a
                              canvas her sister had left behind

    like a hand of
    a clock an egg
    I'll

                              Things Are Ready
                              or Answering Laughter or
                              Are You Passing

    kid pops through porch
    glancing
            slips away
            laughs

                              A Title is another &
                              Titled & then: White
                              Balloon Hidden

    moving over hills
    in silent ripples
    wild brushwork
                  colour-intricacies
    ten then see

            [crystals & grids]

                      & then a slat gave way
                      & you slipped & fell
                      into

the boiling sea (one-two)
between the ship & the quay
(two-three)

                      & yr World or Clique [h'mm
                      haven't decided that one yet]
                      tightens to set tò

amid gambits   crypto-babble
    paper clips   staples
books   papers

                      the flickering shadows
                      of career commentators
                      & their recent acquisitions

among the strangler
fig. snow. a quick
wind bangs

                      yr roof. a slab hits
                      the skylight.

jet-line through
cloud-spot/water-flash/
sea-flash/

                      electrical fizzle
                      between communicating
                      pairs

            how proud we are

      how proud of you
         we are

      how very
        very
      ART

      Bread
      has been
      an important
      food

      ever since man
      first learned how to grind
      cereals into flour.

      The
      earliest
      loaves
      were simple unleavened cakes

      dried in the sun.

      Leavened bread is mentioned
      in the earliest chapters
      of the Bible
      & seems to have been invented
      by the Egyptians.

Splendid & unforgettable are the shrines of the gods

How fine they look in their ancient groves

    Splendid the Gods

    how fine they look

    set round with the Jewel Fence

    an unworldly air

Splendid & unforgettable are the shrines of the gods.
How fine they look in their groves of ancient trees
that wear an unworldly air, set round with the jewel fence
& on the sacred saka tree the white cloth symbol hung.

TWO

How do you do.
Tundish.
Thanks.

le seinm na gcuach ar bhruach
na gcoille go sámh.
O Hope

spread wide your Narrow Hands!

He dropped in   unexpectedly too
had tea (tay)
        2 sugars   black.
                        Steam.

Strange faces reflected upside-down
in the liquid in my cup
the other day.
        (Séamas Dall)

It's an ABC turn it over
look in peer
        down dizzy
                to find

(then crossing the mountains we got stranded one night)

one drunk woman
                far
                    below sway. In the
present. Pattern. BC.

        Moving over old photographs of Avoca
        wistful of the past not that not
        certainly not falls

on a map a timetable a list one egg
two impromptus &
a mark.

Picking persimmon by the waterway
with the health officer
of the brigade.

They loved music vine-spiralling the
trellis she loved the
trellis

he the cross-sections. Avocation. And
regret. Next please. Down. Thank
you.

      I
     dig
    & I-my
     tater
     digs
   & his-his
    tad-tad
     tug
     too
   ho-hum
    swet
     wet
    slap
    coily
    oily
& splasht it
     yep
    said
good ah good
   slippy
    man
    said
    dug

every body
said
yep-yep
petty
gun-squat
yup that
sit
dug
what a pin is
what
uhm
lout
what
un/derlocking
tatty
hoker
yap
yap
snappy
  bang
   of
    the
     boots
    of
    the
obvious
bang
bang
tap dizzy ah
daddy oh
dug
little brittles
with a
new skin
cheap
tap
tap
good
good

Natives were capturing guns runs this narrative while
bad lads in their labs dally as mere
ballads dandle the baby-culture

& slaps together on the sharps: at 52/104
I've had quite enough
Creativity

        Free Expression, Genius & all that.
        Quits.

        Let's communicate.

And entered a private street. Footsteps stretch. As this, then that. Tick/tock. Predatory plumage, & the pen I write with combine on the one vine – let it rain, let it rain – so that by half-past ten I entered my train with my ticket, playing musical instruments. Then gold, then red from a rainbow around our heads (how many anniversaries/how many pebbles make a path out?) the sky shot through with eyes looking up.

More & more this gets on yr nerves (black slab over the bay, porcelain gull-dots that tilt & disappear) until voices: *Ah-ha then Mr Recluse, what's in yr pockets, eh?* Ghost-diktats, paper, gold reserves.

BREAD

I

A sack of white flour fell off a lorry outside a funeral parlour.
There was a funeral in progress. It was raining and the
flour congealed and became slippy. A man with a haversack
on his back crossing the road stepped on a patch of this
porridgy mess…

Whorls of branchlets swept and trailing to the water's rhythm,
the female can be seen as a green oval flask-shaped surprise,
the male spherical orange sculpted exterior that breaks into eight
sections in maturity releasing clouds…

Throwing himself to the side of an on-coming van and into a cyclist's
path, his front wheel jams in a drain, the cyclist lands on the bonnet of
the van, his bicycle topples onto a dog sniffing a wet stain on the back
tyre of a hearse, the van hits a bollard, the cyclist slides off, the haversack-
carrier rolls to safety, an old lady looks round, the funeral's fiscal graphline
rose, the sets were perfect, the lead got up.

The hearse driver looked round. The van driver got out. The bus stopped.
Traffic lights changed red. A goods train trundled by on a bridge
overhead: black/orange, black/orange, black. Frequency times length
equals velocity. Hello? Yes? Splendid! It's a quarter past three, mid-point
in the wave…

        essen   in part
        tiall   by grou
        y a p   pings o
        oem i   f twent
        s a f   y-six q
        lat s   uite we
        urfac   ll-know
        e cov   n-symbo
        ered   ols.

As to each delicate item in the hive yr trivia is as engaging as
my trivia. And sticks. Then palps to the paralysed hymenoptera:
busy busy busy.

or:

a
song
is
a

a
song
is
a

a
song
is
a

sh
ap
e

SONNET

From the nine facts the typist is
Charlotte & the nurse must be Alice.
The hostess lives west of Charlotte &
Doris lives directly north of the typist.
Therefore Doris can't be the hostess.
Putting these results into a small map
it will turn out that Alice lives
four miles south & three miles west of Doris
which by Pythagoras makes the distance
five miles. And Betty, of course, is the hostess.

II

I feel I should feel better now.
Here you will feel better later.
Later   later   even later.
Better later.

wall couple

coop.

don't eat sweets
don't pick your nose
don't piss in yr knickers
                    – the beginning.

&
a
song
is
I was told
shh

stock
blade
bit

shaving some white wood smooth in shadow

step

quite   thank you for that

clouding the egg that develops then
into a dark thick-walled spore

a
  fresh
a
  is
they
  said

not (what?) not so long ago
                            one quiet Saturday
afternoon
          detached

nick
whittle
gouge

a song
they said

note
      don't
do you?
a

sh
ap
e
ah

yes

falling

earth return
earthshine
ear trumpet
earwax
earwig
ease

hammer that home & sell it.

happy art fluid art
who are so
serious

happy art a cow
in experience
daisies

buttercup grass happy
art a vow to
experience

stems earth god's little cow
a bright enamel dot
ambling over

grasses & tested in
the root of yr
fly zoom

e-sus in the sky nested in
for once. happy
art.

sit up. take stock. a leaf
in life rayed
luminous

& glinting in a slight
breeze until
the –

rolling barely over oblong
stain for us inwards
now

& at the power of our breath
again – until
the

              until the
              until the
           Descent to Earth

Quick, turn, disappear under a sliding keel, return, silver, gold-black, green, slipping into many waters many times once on one rival map after another, twining –

step –

the fish rise. Bank to bank. Unravel. Arrive. *YA!* goes this storm in the trees. *YA!* Violins are working hard now. [*YA!*] Is that broken stone down there your oh your *heart?* Life, one backlit bedchamber after another connected by feather-lined corridors in a ring ... Phone me when you get back.

> *cutting*
>
> *or vibrating*
>
> *or light arriving*
>
> *snapping into place*
>
> *multiple as seeds*
>   *in tight array*
>
> *like burning firewood*
>
> *leaves dispersing*
>
> *visiting strangers*
>
> *a dry mudball*
>
> *mixing lacquer*
>
> *spring water welling up*

pulse

    like dusty earth

    like being stopped by a horizontal partition

    like a suspended curtain
    black

    like a sword lying flat
      about to be gripped

    like that

    like a smooth pill

    like glory …

beats a rhythm in dust

    pelvis swaying
    look   like this
      away to
      from to
    shatters &
    re-forms
    it matters & it gathers

    fingertips to the
    (*Nei Ching*)
    of the many links
    so many
    of the many links
    that make up the twisted chain

    in love
    the twisted chain
    "detail
      is all."
          In hate:
    orchestration.

III

but "carry the message"

                              a fat ark under a tree
                              & all that agua rising

who signed
what for whom?
what?   when?

                    in 1803 Hicks & his growing
                    family

the Holy Spirit

                    & the Metropolitan Museum of Art
                    in New York

alterations &
touches

                    a sleepy little village in Ireland
                    then Ennis for godsake after Ha Tulo

under a bluegum tree
        swish & glisten
        not human sacrifice after all for a minute but
not to limit
yrself to Peaceable Kingdom paintings

                                    too/either

            ok then:
            carry one

a tendency
& I see towards
bisymmetry

                              until she was 49 & then
                              only because she found a
                              canvas her sister had left

behind like the hand of
a clock an egg
I'll

                              Things Are Ready
                              or Answering Laughter or
                              Are You Passing

kid pops through porch
glancing
        slips away
        laughs

                              hello ellen. hello helen.
                              have you heard? there's
                              been a horrible accident.

oh dear. what's happened?
hilda higgins' husband
has had an accident

                              on his horse. how awful!
                              is he injured? how did
                              it happen?

A Title is another &
Titled & then: White
Balloon Hidden

> note wild brushwork
> very wristy
> ten then see

crystals & grids

---

                drop stops & the tops
                will crop for themselves

that's five

        I mean tip

                wonderful   may be

                it's a game in hide & seek
                or dip & pursuit/quite formal/
                too   see/saw

six

        said

                sad at supper
                happy by midmorning through
                the following week
                briefly

                spark

BUT/
        in about 1841 for reasons
        so far undiscovered Field
        & his wife, & daughter Henriette,
        moved to New York City

                I'll never now grow up to be
                "an illustrious itinerant limner
                with a bustling career"

flower flowing

                neat in the ell of my trim lapel

CODA

a wisp of smoke from a village on a hilltop

a spider from a lamp

a bird saws   over & over   law-seem   daw-son   drop!

an apple   an egg

black points. gold stars. oily inside upper of a buttercup.

he just came in & sang some songs.

But what a price these Japanese women paid.

one such engraved amulet made of onyx presented to St Alban's Abbey by Aethelred the Unready

In the early days of broadcasting the BBC Advisory Committee on Spoken English helped those "whose daily duty it is to broadcast the world's news"

Scraping Bird   Bird-Twang   Squeak   Fiddle   flit from black to black

gaps   hollows   ridges   organized spaces

But what/this noise, what is it?

Did he say: it's yr mind   or it's *in* yr mind?

This is the first time I (see this film)

In medieval Denmark the custom of tying the skin of a white worm round the waist of the parturient woman prevailed.

to wake up

& resting ... to wake up, without echo, step by step, green domes, gull on a flagpole, in the first place & stop ... but what/ this noise, what is it?

Tig 587

Echo says: you.

    Then it's true?
    Eyes get colder
    & that changes

    the luminous
    instant/cut/
    Bolder sd

    Ominous

    but does it? the sun
    caught on rooftops
    delays us

    a silver dot
    in the sky
    making a bright white

    line

    too a noise
    stormslapped flag
    (& its absence:

    gull on a stone)
    pebbles that click on a wave's recession
    over a beach

    then ...

    So it's true?

Japanese women are not likely to bang a shoe on the table.

All that these able writers have said on language has been challenging, provocative, & generally very helpful.

Thank you.

```
                    clutching a bright
                                    blur of fruit
            your mother gave you
                                        you disappear into
        childhood
                                        over a metal bridge
            & on to a train
                        for school forever.
                                            tact.
                the ceremony begins.
                                    black into white
                                        & back.
    butterflies erupt & disappear over a hedge.
                                        seeds on a single gust
    across the neighbourhood
                                        you circle thus/quick
    where's your pencil?
                        is that a map?
                sails, distant.
                            cliffbase. flecks.
            oily movements
                    in a pear-shaped stone.
                        burst of rain on the roof overhead.
                    that blunt instrument
                                        yr mind.
                the ceremony begins
                        it all begins
                    all of it
                        all begins
                    over again
                            to
                            travel up to
                                let yr eye travel
                            slowly
                            up the stem
                        green
                                up along it
                            in a pocket of light
                            leaves
                        light cilia
                            to the shaped
                            silver in the air
                            then
                                to flowers
                        moving &
                            leaves
                            & the light in them
                                up
                            inhale it
                            pass
                            green
                            blue
                            red
```

Tig 589

then
long branching
stems
with whorls
of branchlets
swept
& trailing
to the
water's
pulse
the female
can be seen
as a green
oval flask-shaped
surprise
    the male
    spherical
    orange
    chiselled exterior
    that breaks into eight
    intricate sections
    in maturity
    releasing clouds…
        clouding
        the egg that
        develops then
        into a
        dark
        thick-walled
        spore
        which falls
        from the plant
        giving
        rise
        in the end
        to a
        new
        startle of

long
thin
branching
stems
that are splendid
                splendid & unforgettable

            grasp sparrow's tail
                        single whip
            play guitar
                        lean forward
            picking persimmon
                        in the backyard
            by the waterway
                        blessing animals
            without panic
                        white crane
            spreads its
                        wings
            brush knee & twist
                        step
            brush knee & fix
                        step
            step forward
                        to the waterway
            with the health
                        officer of the brigade
            small intricate
                        sounds   bread
            descent to earth
                        a falling leaf
            migrating butterflies
                        white balloon hidden

            grasp sparrow's tail
                        single whip
            play guitar
                        lean forward
            white crane
                        spreads its wings
            brush knee
                        & twist –
            step –
                        play guitar
            brush knee
                        & fix – step –

                                                Tig 593

step forward
> deflect
downward
> intercept &
punch
> draw back

(split) & push

windshield wipers
> a pale finger
on cold glass
> in the rain
dusty steel
> grainy wash
bubbles in a
> bathtub
clouds in
> patterns
winds
> leaves
day/night
> spinning &
dissolving
> trickling
down to
> roots whose
roots
> have roots
& connect
> in a vivid
zigzag of
> changing
agreements
> in a glaze
below
> the surface
you lately
> reached through

to.
           touched.
but …

dandelion & daisy

cross hands

dandelion & daisy begin

cross hands

cross hands folding.

Beginning of an answer

Beginning of calling

Beginning of slaying

Sustenance of bees

Beauty of eyebrows

Lustre of eye-light

Beginning of honey

CODA CODA

CODA CODA

[A PLACE.
TO STAY]

tools made from
bric-a-brac this
& that the river
gave up

you were ending
your circle a
littered track
of extravagant

things a tiny
garden at the back
run wild a neat
platform set in

the fork of a
sycamore over a
stream to sink
your water bucket

in your face in
the sky as you
dreamed that mild
losing interlock

of the made with
the growing put
through your wry
smile dreaming …

tishhh go cars on
wet streets filter-
ing yellow through
dense scaffolding

casting black on
black from rainwind
in waves outside –
shadowy – midnight –

mind your head –
place your foot –
who's there?

one night on
the roof watching
scattered

light-sparkle on the
hills around the city
your boot cracked open a

sheet of pale blue
polystyrene to fall
suddenly through
the dark but: pulled

back. stopped short:
   terrified.

   then.

migrating butterflies

blessing the animals

picking persimmon

bit by bit/the whole
spread rising structure
wooden arcs spiral
staircase ornate clock.

   the ant
   moves the
   grain.

                    then left out
                                refuse
        head touched canopy
                                    clouds of greenfly
            nodded to
                    neighbours
                                stepped in back
                                                for more bags
    slight discomfort in the left
                            foot (Tuesday)
bus goes by
                                    dog slips in
                    pushed handle
                                down through hallway
            then turned to close
                            the

                    otherwise/
                    Migrating
                        Butterflies
                    Blessing the
                    Animals Picking
                    Persimmon A
                    Falling Leaf
                        /// Descent
                    to Earth Panic
                    Backyard A
                    Sparrow A
                    Title Tig Bread
                    White Balloon
                    Hidden Health
                    Officer of the
                    Brigade   Cockfight
                        Waterway   A Place to
                    Stay   Always   Always

Dandelion & daisy begin.

Soon a sweetish whiff

of wallflower & walks

past the Ashtown Tin Box Factory

down to the pouring canal.

1981–2006

NOTES

Some snippets of the Irish Language (*Gaeilge*), appear in the text.

p 126: *Ní féasta go rósta, ní céasa go pósadh*: Marriage is difficult. Literally: 'no feast without a roast, no marriage without a crucifixion.'

p: 223: *Fadó:* long ago.

p. 224: *Tús maith*: a good beginning.

p 233: *i ngile an tráthnóna, i mainistir na feola*: in the afternoon light, in the monastery of the flesh, from the poem *Siollabadh* ('Syllabling') by Seán Ó Ríordáin (1916–1977).

p 237: *raghaidh mé síos ag lorg daoirse:* I'll go down looking for servitude.

p 237: *Is raghaidh mé síos anocht:* And I'll go down tonight.

p 237: *Ó fadfad libh de ló is d'oíche. Is beidh mé íseal is beidh mé dílis d'bhur snabsmaointe:* Oh I'll stay with you day & night & I'll be humble & I'll be faithful to yr snob-thoughts. From the poem *Saoirse* (Freedom) by Seán Ó Ríordáin. My 'translations' of Ó Ríordáin in *Things That Happen* are deliberately distorted.

p 252: *Do-chum glóire Dé is onóra na h-Éireann*: For the glory of God & the honour of Ireland. Motto of *The Irish Press* newspaper.

p 253: *nóinín, neantóg, bainne bó bleacht, feochadán, sabhaircín, fraoch*: daisy, nettle, cowslip, thistle, primrose, heather.

p 253: *fite fuaite ... An tosach, ar deireadh*: closely interwoven ... The beginning, at last.

p 257: *Gósta garbh-Bhéarla*: smattering of pidgin English.

p 257: *wisha-wisha*: to echo the Irish exclamation *mhuise* (pronounced 'wisha'): well! indeed! as well as Enid Blyton.

p 273: epigraph to *Steps: ... agus a haon, dó, trí*: ... & one, two, three.

p 314: *Aisling*: vision poem with a political edge.

p 328: *seafóideach*: silly, nonsensical.

p 362: *Oifig an Phoist*: Post office. The 'impossible accent' is a '*fada*', or long accent, used over vowels only.

p 362: *Éist! Éist liom!*: Listen! Listen to me!

p 430: *dofheicthe*: invisible, as minority languages can be.

p 434: *le seinm na gcuach ar bhruach na gcoille go sámh*: with the cuckoo's peaceful singing on the edge of the wood (Séamas Dall MacCuarta, 1650?–1733).

p 455: *súgán*: straw rope.

p 502: *Dáil*: the Irish parliament.

p 509: *Tig*: house.

p 521: *Deoir*: tear; *deoir fhearthainne*: raindrop. These meanings latent in stanzas 7/8:

different (or) touching a windowpane where
drops gather ( ) difference ( ) &
or different

( ) colours even ...

p 533: *An Ceangal*: L'envoi.

p 540: *béarlagair*: jargon.

pp 494, 549 & 595 (final 7 lines); *briatharogham* ('Boast of women' 'Assembly of hounds', 'Beginning of an answer' etc): cryptic 2-word glosses (in Irish) on Ogham letter-names in medieval mss, but much older than these sources. Meant to be mnemonic.

Sesotho

Some snippets of Sesotho occur in the text:

p 125: The crowded buses plying the mountainous kingdom of Lesotho in the 1980s were manufactured in apartheid regime South Africa by a company called United Bodies. They bore the company's plaque on the back.

p 126: *Tebang*: village birth-place of the then Queen of Lesotho.

p 137: *ke ha ha kereke*: I build a church (a missionary hymn).

p 146: *koro*: wheat, but here used to represent the rippled sound of water flowing.

p 146: *ka marao*: behind.

*

p 121: 'twirling the edge': street traders' term for giving 'bargains' to customers in front to draw others in from the back.

p 129: 'these are the kinds of dreams I have': Robert Lax on Patmos.

p 497: *Tzuba* is an imaginary language.

Tig: Titles in square brackets are those of naïve paintings, along with some others – A Title, Titled, Things Are Ready, Descent to Earth, White Balloon Hidden, Answering Laughter, etc – filtered into the body of the book throughout.

https://mauricescullysite.wordpress.com

Author photo: James Keating.

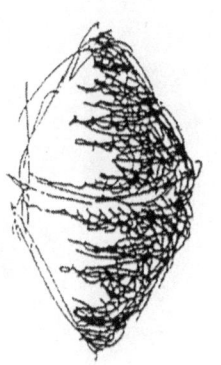

www.ingramcontent.com/pod-product-compliance
Lightning Source LLC
Chambersburg PA
CBHW031407230426
43668CB00007B/236